CoderDojo
<NANO>

CREATE WITH <CODE>

MAKE YOUR OWN GAME

SCHOLASTIC

‹PRESS START›

This book is about coding games. It could be the first step you'll take toward becoming a great coder. And, if you're interested in games, or coding in general, then CoderDojo has lots to offer.

With the help of this book, you're going to make a real video game. You'll create animations for your character and robotic enemies. You'll learn the in-game physics of a 2D platform game. You'll even create scores and game-over screens for a truly awesome gaming experience.

We'll be following along with the Nanonauts, a group of friends who want to make their very own video game too! They'll be learning all about **JavaScript**, a programming language used to create games and programs for web browsers. You can learn these skills too so that you and your friends can make your own awesome games to play and share!

The Nanonauts are part of CoderDojo, a coding club for young people that lets you hang out with other coders, learn new stuff, and generally have fun with computers. Dojos are run by volunteers all around the world. They are free to attend and you work with your friends. If you're lucky, there may be a Dojo near you; you may have even been to one before! To see if there is a Dojo near you, visit **coderdojo.com** and enter your location.

If there isn't a Dojo near you, don't worry. You can just start your own official mini-Dojo, a Dojo Nano. How? It's easy.

Ingredients for a Dojo Nano:

- ☯ **one or more friends**

- ☯ **a computer**

- ☯ **this book**

IDEAS + FRIENDS + CODE = DOJO NANO

PROGRAM INTRODUCTION

The Nanonauts are a group of friends who love to play video games. They play everything from sports and racers to platformers and adventure games. They always have great ideas for games, so one day they decided to make their own!

In this book, we're going to learn how to write programs using a programming language called **JavaScript**. Our program will be a simple "endless runner" game, and it will run inside your web browser.

We're going to build the program very slowly, almost line by line, so you have a chance to understand why each line is there. At any time, don't be afraid to experiment! Change values, change graphics, put lines in different places, see what happens. Save regular copies of your work, then you can always go back to an earlier version.

If something doesn't work at first, don't get discouraged. Look at your code carefully and see if you can spot where it's not working. Programmers call that **debugging**. If you ever get completely stuck, be sure to check out our website for tips, tricks, and coding examples: **scholastic.com/coder-dojo**

FIRST PROGRAM

This is the code for our first program. Don't worry if you don't understand it just yet. Type the code into a simple **plain-text editor** such as Notepad (Windows), Caret (Chromebook), or GEdit (Ubuntu), or in a **code editor** such as TextWrangler (macOS) or Notepad++ (Windows). Make sure you type the code exactly as it's written here. If you're not sure how to do this, go to scholastic.com/coder-dojo/texteditors. If you're using a code editor, check this out for some useful tips: scholastic.com/coder-dojo/codeeditor

```
<!DOCTYPE html>
<html>
<head>
<title>Nanonaut Action</title>
</head>
<body>
<script>
console.log('Hello World!');
</script>
</body>
</html>
```

Your code should look something like this when typed into a text editor.

```
                                          program.html

  nanonauts              program.html              ✕

                    1    <!DOCTYPE html>
                    2    <html>
                    3    <head>
                    4    <title>Nanonaut Action</title>
                    5    </head>
                    6    <body>
                    7    <script>
                    8    console.log('Hello World!');
                    9    </script>
                    10   </body>
                    11   </html>

 /desktop/nanonauts/program.html                              LF  UTF-8  HTML
```

Make a folder on your computer called **nanonauts** and save the code file as **program.html**.

nanonauts

program.html

The code tells a web browser, such as Chrome or Firefox, what to do. Double-click the file to open it up in your web browser. If all goes well, you should see ... nothing.

What? Why? It says something about "Hello World!" in the code, so why can't we see it in the browser? Well, we didn't actually tell the browser to display anything where we can normally see it.

NINJA TIP

Some word-processing programs will automatically turn your quote marks (") into "smart quotes" (","). Your code won't work! Always use a plain-text editor.

MORE ONLINE

If you need help opening and saving code files, go to scholastic.com/coder-dojo/openfiles

OPENING THE CONSOLE

So where can we see it? It's time to look at an extremely important tool when you're programming in the browser: the **console**.

Here are some ways you can open the console in all of the major browsers:

In Firefox, open the **Tools** menu, then under **Web Developer** select **Web Console**.

Tools | Window | Help

Downloads
Add-ons
Sign In To Sync...

Web Developer ▶
Page Info

Toggle Tools
Inspector
Web Console
Debugger
Style Editor
Performance
Network

Developer Toolbar
WebIDE
Browser Console
Responsive Design Mode
Eyedropper
Scratchpad
Service Workers
Page Source

Get More Tools

In Chrome, open the **View** menu, then under **Developer** select **JavaScript Console**.

View | History | Bookmarks | People | Window | Help

Always Show Bookmarks Bar
Always show Toolbar in full screen

Stop
Force Reload This Page

Enter Full Screen
Actual Size
Zoom In
Zoom Out

Encoding
Developer ▶

View Source
Developer Tools
JavaScript Console

In Microsoft Internet Explorer or Microsoft Edge, press **F12** to open a window with all of the developer tools, then select the **Console** tab in that window.

Console	Watch	Locals	Call stack	Breakpoints

In Safari on macOS, open the **Safari** menu and select **Preferences**. Under the **Advanced** tab make sure **Show Develop Menu in Menu Bar** is switched on and close the preferences again. Then open the **Develop** menu and select **Show Error Console**.

Develop	Window	Help

Open Page With ▶
User Agent ▶

Enter Responsive Design Mode
Show Snippet Editor
Show Extension Builder

Connect Web Inspector
Show Error Console
Show Page Source
Show Page Resources

Start Timeline Recording
Start Element Selection

Empty Caches
Disable Caches

Disable Images
Disable Styles
Disable Javascript
Disable Extensions
Disable Site-specific Hacks

| Elements | Console | Sources | Network | Timeline | Profiles |

Hello World!   program.html:8

THERE IT IS!

LEVEL UP!
You created and used your first program!

WORDS TO REMEMBER

Code editor – A program that allows you to edit code. You don't have to use a special code editor – Notepad works just fine – but code editors make it easier by color-coding the markup and providing other helpful features.

Edit – When you make changes to code, you edit it.

File – Whenever you save anything onto your computer or up to the web, it's stored as a file. Files can contain any kind of information – they can be web pages, images, songs, PDF documents, you name it. But programmers refer to all of these things as files.

File name – Files always have a file name. Our file is called `program.html`. File names usually end with a period followed by three or four letters (such as `.png`, `.pdf`, `.html`). This is known as a **file extension**, and it tells the computer what kind of file it is. For example, a `.png` file is an image file.

Folder – When you save a file, it goes into a folder. A folder is a particular storage location on a computer. Folders can contain other folders. You refer to a folder by giving its **path**. For example, `C:\nanonauts` gives the path to the **nanonauts** folder on your computer's **C:** drive that contains `program.html`.

Web browser – Chrome, Firefox, Internet Explorer, Opera, Safari, and other applications that let you browse the web are called web browsers. It's also used to view the JavaScript console.

Console – This is one of the tools to help you develop programs and websites inside your browser. It shows you output from the current web page, and also allows you to enter JavaScript code for immediate execution.

NINJA TIP

Save copies of your code as you work your way through the book. You can check changes, and if something goes wrong, you can load the last saved file and not have to redo the work.

USING THE CONSOLE

All of the programming we're going to do happens between the **<script>** lines, using a programming language called JavaScript. All modern browsers understand this language. You can change the text between the quote marks of the code to display a different message in the console. Try changing the code to this:

```
console.log('The Nanonauts rock!');
```

---

program.html

> 📁 nanonauts

program.html ✕

```
1    <!DOCTYPE html>
2    <html>
3    <head>
4    <title>Nanonaut Action</title>
5    </head>
6    <body>
7    <script>
8    console.log('The Nanonauts rock!');
9    </script>
10   </body>
11   </html>
```

/desktop/nanonauts/program.html   LF   UTF-8   HTML

Save the file, then refresh the page in the browser. The console should now say "The Nanonauts rock!"

Elements | Console | Sources | Network | Timeline | Profiles | ✕

The Nanonauts rock!   program.html:8

Now change the code to:

```
console.log('this is wrong
```

When you refresh, the console will show something like this:

> 🛑 ▶ SyntaxError: Unexpected EOF

This means we typed something the computer didn't understand. This will happen a lot! That's why the console is so important: It allows the computer to tell us what went wrong, so we can help fix it.

Computers are good at math. Change the code to those examples to see the answers in the console:

```
console.log(5 + 2);
```

```
console.log(5 - 2);
```

```
console.log(5 * 2);
```

7

> console.log(5 + 2);

3

> console.log(5 - 2);

10

> console.log(5 * 2);

```
console.log(5 / 2);
```

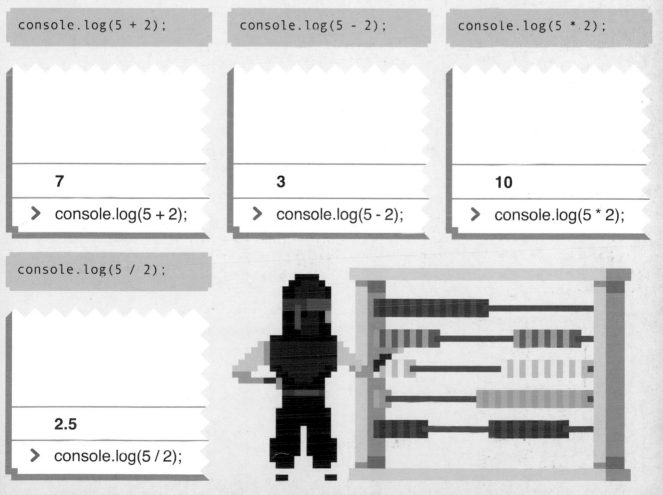

2.5

> console.log(5 / 2);

VARIABLES

Computers don't just calculate values; they can also store them so we can use them later. This is extremely important. We do this with **variables**. Variables are like a box you can put a value in. Variables have names, so you can refer to them later. And you can change the value in the variable at any time. Let's have a look.

Change the code between the script tags to:

```
var value1 = 5;
var value2 = 2;
console.log(value1 + value2);
```

The **syntax** of a variable, or the order in which it's written, is simple. Here's an example to show each part:

keyword	variable name	assignment	value	semicolon
var	value1	=	5	;

NINJA TIP

Semicolons will tell the computer where one command (also called a **statement**) ends and the next one begins, so be careful about putting them in!

You will see "7" again. You've told the browser "Put 5 in this variable called **value1**, and 2 in this other variable called **value2**, then add them together."

Now add the following under the last **console.log** line:

```
var value3 = 1;
console.log(value1 - value3);
```

Refresh the page in the browser and you'll see "7" and "4." Do you understand why the browser showed a 4?

Now change the first line to: `var value1 = 4;`

Refresh and you will see "6" and "3." Without variables, you would have had to make lots of changes to see these new results.

The first time you use a variable, you have to **declare** it with the **var** keyword. That way the computer understands you want to use a new variable. Without **var** it will look around for a variable with the same name, and complain if it can't find it.

You can change variables after you've declared them – that's why they're called variables. Try this next code. Notice how we set the value of the variable again, without using the **var** keyword, on the third line.

The code executes in the order it is written, so the first **console.log** line will output **value1** as 5, then we change **value1** before the final **console.log** line:

```
var value1 = 5;
console.log(value1);
value1 = 4;
console.log(value1);
```

You can also copy values from one variable to another, like the second line in this code:

```
var value1 = 5;
var value2 = value1 + 1;
value1 = 4;
console.log(value1);
console.log(value2);
```

CAN YOU GUESS WHAT THE BROWSER WILL SHOW?

STRINGS

Variables can be more than just numbers. For instance, they can also be text. We call those **strings**, because they're like a string of single characters. Add this line to your code:

```
var name = "Nanonauts!";
```

The computer knows it's a string because you used the single quote marks. You can also use double quotes, which is useful if you want to use an apostrophe in a string. Make sure you use the same kind of quotes at the beginning and the end:

```
var message = "I can't believe how good they are.";
```

You can add strings together too:

```
console.log(name + message);
```

NINJA TIP

If you want to try a line of code really quickly, you don't need to edit, save, and refresh. You can also just type it in at the bottom of the browser console.

Nanonauts! I can't believe how good they are.

> console.log(name + message);

Variable names can be a combination of:

- ☯ Any letter from the Western alphabet (without accents), upper- or lowercase.

- ☯ Any number.

- ☯ The underscore ("_") or the dollar ("$") character.

But they cannot start with a number, and they cannot be the same as a keyword.

The most important thing about variable names: They're for **you** and other people who read and work with the code. It makes no difference to the computer if a variable is called **myAge** or **xrgl$$3**. But the first one is much easier to read, and you could probably guess that variable contained an age. The second one doesn't make sense to a person reading it.

THINGS TO DO NEXT

Try creating a variable called **var** or **function** – both are keywords in JavaScript. What does the browser say?

LEVEL UP!

You've learned how to store numbers and text in variables!

UTILIZING APIs

Seeing things happen in the console is all well and good, but it's more interesting to make things happen on-screen. Let's look at how to do that. Remove the code from between the `<script>` lines and write:

```
var canvas = document.createElement('canvas');
canvas.width = 800;
canvas.height = 600;
document.body.appendChild(canvas);
```

There's a lot going on in these four lines. We're going to look at them in more detail. We'll also be revisiting the concepts many times later on in this book, so don't worry if something is not immediately clear.

Let's look at the syntax of the first line:

keyword	variable name	assign	object variable	dot operator	function call	function parameter
var	canvas	=	document	.	createElement	('canvas')

Where did this **document** variable come from? We didn't create it: There's no **var document** anywhere. The browser has created it for us before our code begins to run. Through an **object** – a type of variable that stores values together, like **document** and **console** – we can ask the browser what's going on or tell it what to do. The people making browsers have agreed what happens when **console.log** or **document.createElement** is written. This agreement is an Application Programming Interface, or **API**.

The dot between **document** and **createElement** is called the **dot operator**. Here, we're saying "We want to access something called **createElement** from the object called **document**."

A **function** is a piece of code that we can **call** in order to get things done – **createElement** is a function we've used. Functions are great for taking bits of code and isolating them, so we can call that code more than once and we don't have to copy it everywhere. We'll be writing our own functions later in this book.

If, for instance, we have a function that counts how many words there are in a string of text, it needs to have that text to work with. The function expects that text as a **parameter**, and we pass it that parameter between **parentheses**. That's how you can tell **createElement()** here is a function: because of the parentheses after the name.

We pass a parameter to the **createElement** function: **'canvas'**, a string.

So what does this **createElement** function that belongs to the **document** object actually do? It has a reasonably clear name: This function creates a new **element**, of the type **canvas**. A web page – what the browser calls a document – consists of different kinds of elements: text, buttons, footers, and so on.

NINJA TIP

If you want to find out more about these elements, look at a language called **HTML**. HTML is used to define web pages, just like we did on page 8. If you want to learn more about HTML, look out for *CoderDojo Nano: Create With Code – Build Your Own Website*.

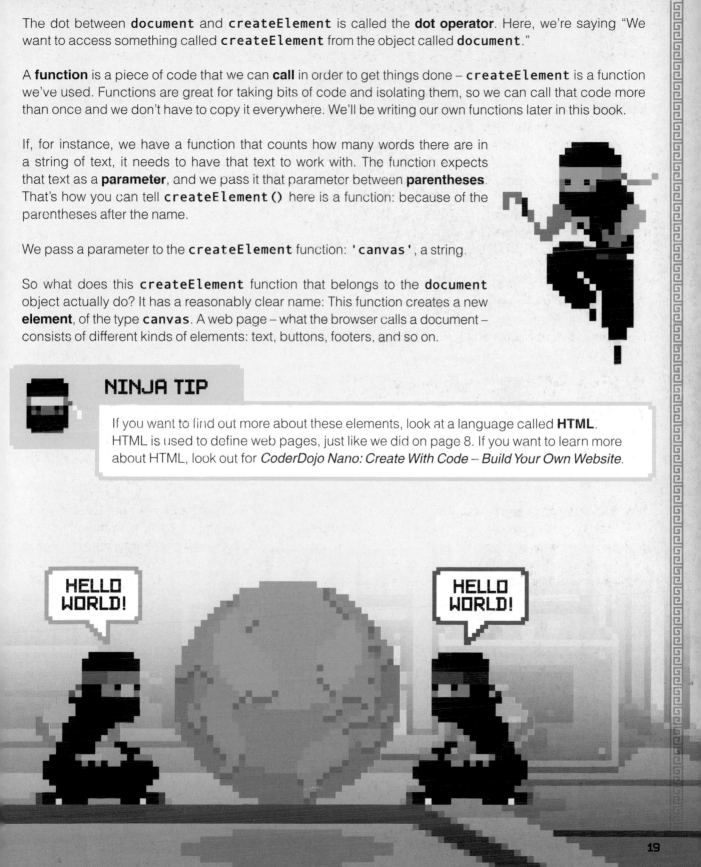

A **canvas** is one kind of web page element. It's a rectangular area that we can draw on, and that's what we'll be doing in the rest of the book.

So we call `createElement`, which is a function the browser puts at our disposal. This function creates a new **canvas** element and then returns an object for us to use, which represents this new canvas. We need to assign the object to a variable name, or we won't be able to use it.

NINJA TIP

How do we know the variable **document** has a function called `createElement` that takes a string parameter, creates a new HTML element, and returns an object? You'll pick it up as you go along, and you can always look up functions, variables, and more online. A helpful resource for this is Mozilla Developer Network: https://developer.mozilla.org/en-US/

Wow! All that for one line! We'll be using functions, objects, and APIs again and again, so don't worry if you don't understand everything now.

We've asked the browser to create a **canvas** element, but we haven't said how big it should be. So the next two lines set the width and height of the canvas. The object in the **canvas** variable has values named **width** and **height** (again, this is something everyone has agreed on for the API), and we can simply assign new values to them:

```
canvas.width = 800;
canvas.height = 600;
```

We're using **pixels** to measure width and height – a pixel is the smallest dot you can draw on the screen. Our canvas will be 800 pixels wide and 600 pixels high.

Finally, while we have created the canvas, we have not told the browser where it should appear on the current web page. So we use the dot operator to get to the document's **body** element, which is the HTML element that represents everything visible, and then we tell that element to add the canvas to itself using the **appendChild** function:

```
document.body.appendChild(canvas);
```

WORDS TO REMEMBER

HTML – The language used to describe a web page. You can do lots with HTML, but we will only use it a little in this book to set up a simple web page to embed our JavaScript code in.

API – An API is an agreement on how to call or access functions and values in another piece of code. In this book, we're only concerned with the browser's APIs, which say "If you call this function or read this variable, so and so will happen."

Functions – Programs are organized into functions, independent bits of code that ideally do one clearly defined thing. This makes programs easier to understand. Functions help us avoid writing the same code more than once by using a **function call**. Just put it in a function and you can call it as many times as you like. **myFunction()** calls a function named **myFunction**, which means the code inside that function is executed, and then the program continues after the call.

Parameters – Functions may require values so they know what to do. These values are called parameters. For instance, a function that calculates which day of the week someone was born needs a birthday to work with.

Return values – Functions can **return** a value. For instance, a function that calculates which day of the week someone was born would return that day using the **return** command.

Objects – Ways of bundling values or functions together into one thing. These values "belong" to the object: They are its **properties**.

Dot operator – The dot operator allows us to access a value or function belonging to an object. **myPet.age** looks for and returns the value called **age** from the object **myPet**.

Methods – These are functions that belong to an object. We won't be creating our own methods in this book, but we do use methods provided by the browser's APIs. You call them using the dot operator. **myPet.feed()** calls a function named **feed** that belongs to the object **myPet**.

PAINTING ON A CANVAS

OK, so there's a canvas, but it's empty. Let's fix that. Add the following to your code:

```
var c = canvas.getContext('2d');
c.fillStyle = 'green';
c.fillRect(10, 10, 30, 30);
document.body.appendChild(canvas);
```

Now you should see a green square!

What did we do there? We can't talk directly to the canvas, so **getContext('2d')** gives us something known as a **context**, which we need to do something useful with the canvas. Because it's not really important, we simply name the variable **c**. We use **c** from that point onward as a shorthand to access the canvas.

Here, we apply a style to **c** saying "From now on, whatever you draw, color it in green."

```
c.fillStyle = 'green';
```

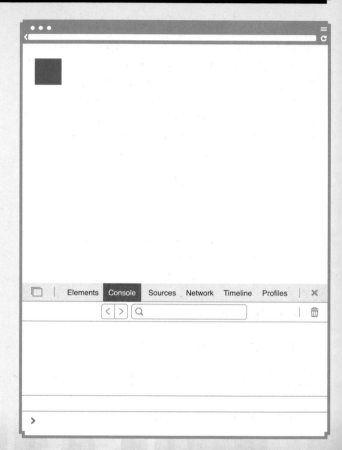

NINJA TIP

As you work through this book, note that new lines added to the code are **bold**. The lines that aren't bold should already be in the code and are to help you position new lines correctly.

THINGS TO DO NEXT

Try replacing the color in **fillStyle** to see how it looks. Try different values for the **fillRect** function parameters.

22

Before we go through the final line in detail, let's look at **coordinate systems**.

Coordinates are references to grid positions. In programming, it's a grid of pixels. The grid begins at 0 in the top left and extends horizontally along the **X-axis** and vertically on the **Y-axis**. This example shape is measured from the top-left square, which is positioned at 10,10. We then measure the width of the shape, which is 30 pixels, and the height, which is also 30 pixels:

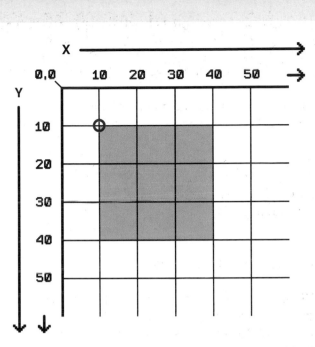

```
c.fillRect(10, 10, 30, 30);
```

In our code, we ask the browser to draw a filled square using function parameters to dictate its placement. The **fillRect** function takes four parameters, all of which are measured in pixels:

1. the X coordinate of the top-left corner of the rectangle

2. the Y coordinate of the top-left corner of the rectangle

3. the width of the rectangle

4. the height of the rectangle

23

LOADING DATA

Drawing rectangles is a start, but for our game we want to use images that we've created with art tools or downloaded from the Internet. Those images are stored in individual files, and we need to tell the browser how to load them.

Telling the browser to load an image file is quite easy but, while it's loading images, our code will actually continue to run. In fact, our code is already running before the web page it is part of has finished loading! So there are multiple things happening at the same time, which can get confusing. If we want to draw an image that hasn't been loaded yet, we won't see anything! So we have to make sure everything we need is there before we continue.

MORE ONLINE

You can download the images we've used in this game at scholastic.com/coder-dojo/gameimages

Save these images into your nanonauts folder, where you've saved the program.html file, to make the game that the Nanonauts are building!

nanonauts

    animatedNanonaut.png

    animatedRobot.png

    background.png

    bush1.png

    bush2.png

    nanonaut.png

We've already seen how you can call a function: You use its name and then add the function's parameters in parentheses, separated by commas. Now we're going to define our own! Add these function lines around the **c.fillStyle** and **c.fillRect** lines:

```
function start() {
c.fillStyle = 'green';
c.fillRect(10, 10, 30, 30);
}
```

This defines a function called **start**, which takes no parameters. Everything between the **braces** (**{}**) is the body, which is executed when we call the function. In this case, it draws a green rectangle.

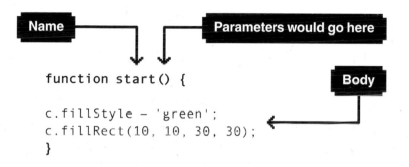

```
function start() {

    c.fillStyle - 'green';
    c.fillRect(10, 10, 30, 30);
    }
```

Name

Parameters would go here

Body

Since we don't actually call this function yet, it's a bit pointless. But before we can call it, we need to make it wait for the images to load before it can execute properly.

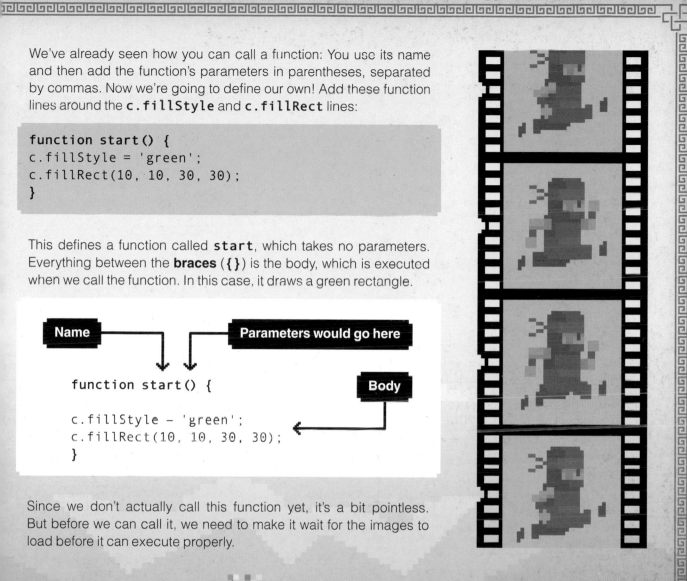

NINJA TIP

Usually when you write code, you'll use **indentation**. This adds space at the beginning of lines to make parts of the code clearer, like the body of a function. Check out scholastic.com/coder-dojo/indentation to see how indentation is implemented.

LOADING THE IMAGES

To make the function wait for images to load we need to ask the browser to let us know when it has finished loading. Insert the following line of code:

```
window.addEventListener('load', start);

function start() {
c.fillStyle = 'green';
```

We're using a browser API again, which is calling a function on the object called **window**. When the browser has finished loading images, it will **trigger** a **load** event and call anyone who wants to know. With this line, we're saying "Please call our **start** function when the load event happens." This will make the browser call our **start** function at the right time.

This is called **event handling**, and it's a common way for different parts of a program to communicate. There are a lot of different kinds of events defined in the browser API, most of which we won't need in this book. Later we will see the **keydown** and **keyup** events that allow us to react to the player pressing keys.

NINJA TIP

Because our **start** function is being called back by other code, we sometimes call this kind of function a **callback**.

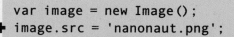

On to images! We're going to be using a few different images for our project. You can use the ones that we've used, or you can change them, make your own, or find other images on the Internet. You can see more about changing the images on page 93.

Put the image files in the **nanonauts** folder you made at the start of the project, then add the following lines to your code:

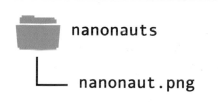

```
var image = new Image();
image.src = 'nanonaut.png';

window.addEventListener('load', start);

function start() {
c.fillStyle = 'green';
c.fillRect(10, 10, 30, 30);
c.drawImage(image, 20, 40);
}
```

First we create an **Image** object, which is an object from the browser API that represents an image. Rather than letting a function create this object for us, like we did with `document.createElement()`, we are creating it directly using the **new** command. In both cases, we end up with an object.

Then we tell the image where to look for its image file. This will make the browser look next to your HTML file for a file called **nanonaut.png**, and it will load that in.

Finally, once we're sure the image has been loaded, we draw it at coordinates 20, 40. And that's all!

NINJA TIP

The API contains **canvas**, **Image**, and other objects, and details what they can be used for.

LEVEL UP!

Now you know how to create shapes and images in a program.

THINGS TO DO NEXT

Try changing the coordinates to see what happens.

SETTING UP A LOOP

Drawing stuff is pretty fun, but making that stuff move is even more fun! To do that, we need to draw something, change it a little bit, draw it again, change it again, endlessly, in a **loop**. We need to do that very quickly, or our eyes won't think it's moving.

To do this, add an **x** and **y** variable, replace the body of the **start** function and create a function called **loop**, as shown below:

```
var x = 0;
var y = 40;

window.addEventListener('load', start);

function start() {
window.requestAnimationFrame(loop);
}

function loop() {
// Drawing code will go here.
window.requestAnimationFrame(loop);
}
```

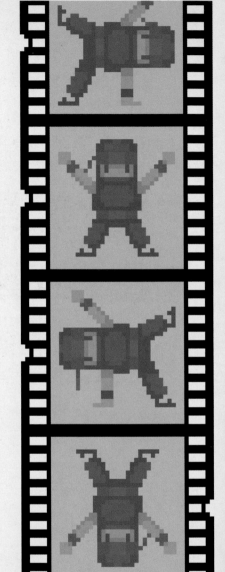

NINJA TIP

The line that starts with **//** is a **comment**. Comments are important, because they help you and other people remember what the code does. Write comments for humans, not for computers!

The **requestAnimationFrame** API call tells the browser we want to draw an animation, and that it should call our loop function at the right time. At the end of the loop, we ask the browser to call us again in the next frame. Otherwise the function would only be called once. By doing this, our loop function is executed 60 times per second, known as **frames per second** (or **FPS**), which creates smooth movement.

At the start of the loop function, replace the comment line with:

```
function loop() {
c.drawImage(image, x, y);
x = x + 1;

window.requestAnimationFrame(loop);
}
```

Run it, and you will see ... a smeared image.

Can you guess why? It's because we're drawing one image on top of the next, time and time again. Before the **drawImage** call, add this:

```
function loop() {
c.clearRect(0, 0, 800, 600);
c.drawImage(image, x, y);
```

This clears a rectangular area of the size of the whole canvas. And now we have a moving Nanonaut.

GAME ON!

Let's build a small game! It's going to be an **endless runner**, a game where you control a character who runs by themselves. It will be simple, but it's the perfect intro to the basics of programming JavaScript.

Here is the list of things we need to make happen in our game:

1.   We see a Nanonaut in an exciting world.

2.   The Nanonaut will fall to the ground.

3.   The Nanonaut can jump into the air.

4.   The Nanonaut automatically runs to the right, followed by the camera.

5.   The Nanonaut is animated.

6.   There are background objects, to make the world more lively.

7.   Evil animated robots run from right to left.

8.   When the robots run off the left side of the screen, they disappear.
   New robots appear on the right.

9.   When the Nanonaut touches a robot, they lose health.

10.   When the Nanonaut has lost all health, the game stops.

Before we go on, we should do some preparations, so we won't run into trouble when our program gets bigger.

First of all, we're going to divide our program into sections using comments, to keep things clear in our heads.

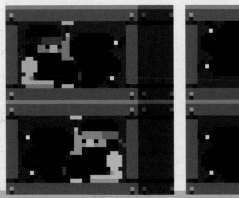

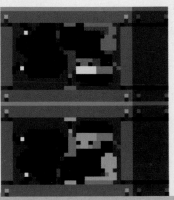

Remove all the code between the `<script>` tags, and add the comments on the right into your code. These comments divide the program up into sections. By writing these comments in uppercase, they stand out from the rest of the code and are easy to locate if you run into trouble.

Next, let's look at what each of the sections will be for.

```
// CONSTANTS
// SETUP
// MAIN LOOP
// PLAYER INPUT
// UPDATING
// DRAWING
```

THE CODE SECTIONS

We are going to use the **CONSTANTS** section to declare variables that we know won't change.

That may seem odd. Why use a variable if it will never change? Why not use the value alone? There are two reasons, and once again they have nothing to do with the browser, but with making our lives easier.

Let's say our canvas is 800 pixels wide. Whenever we need the canvas width, we could just write **800**, as we have done so far. But we may need to calculate, for example, the canvas width minus the width of our Nanonaut. Let's say that's 680. We could just use **680** whenever we need it.

But now imagine we want to make our canvas wider to fit a different screen size. First we need to hunt for every instance of **800** in our program and replace it, hoping there are no values that are also **800** that have nothing to do with canvas width. We also need to remember we did math based on **800**, like the **680** we calculated above, and redo the math, then replace those values. **680** is what we call a **magic number**: It works, but now we can't see what it means or why it's **680** or how we got there.

For example, it's better to do this (you don't need to add these lines to your code):

```
var CANVAS_WIDTH = 800;
var NANONAUT_WIDTH = 120;

var nanonautX = CANVAS_WIDTH - NANONAUT_WIDTH;
```

We're using capital letters to remind us (not the browser, it doesn't care) that this is a constant.

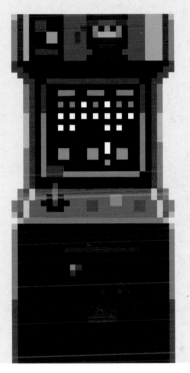

Now it's easy to make the canvas wider, or the Nanonaut slimmer. We are going to put all constant variables like this in the **CONSTANTS** section.

The **SETUP** section will contain everything we need before the game can get going, like setting the canvas size using constants, and loading images. It will also include the declarations of all of the variables that are used in the entire program. The last thing that will happen in this section is setting up the game's main loop.

The **MAIN LOOP** section is where all the keyboard handling, updating, and drawing happens, so you'd think it'd be huge. In fact it will be quite small, because we're going to break all of those things up into functions that go in other sections. Long functions get confusing, so we will break them up into small parts that we can easily understand. The browser will still treat them the same way.

The **PLAYER INPUT** section will contain callbacks, which you may remember are just functions, which are called when the player presses a key.

Inside the **UPDATING** section we will put all of the code that looks at what is happening and which keys the player is pressing, and updates things like positions and score.

Finally, the **DRAWING** section looks at what the previous section has calculated and draws everything in the browser.

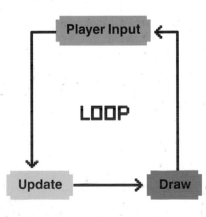

THE FIRST LINES

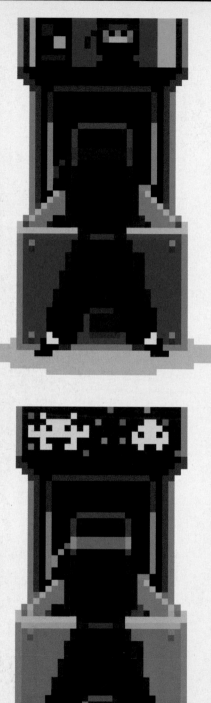

We're going to add the skeleton of the code for our game now. Some things we've seen already, but don't worry if some parts are unfamiliar – we'll look at each section in detail shortly.

Put these lines in your **CONSTANTS** section:

```
var CANVAS_WIDTH = 800;
var CANVAS_HEIGHT = 600;
var NANONAUT_WIDTH = 181;
var NANONAUT_HEIGHT = 229;
var GROUND_Y = 540;
```

This goes in your **SETUP** section:

```
var canvas = document.createElement('canvas');
var c = canvas.getContext('2d');
canvas.width = CANVAS_WIDTH;
canvas.height = CANVAS_HEIGHT;
document.body.appendChild(canvas);

var nanonautImage = new Image();
nanonautImage.src = 'nanonaut.png';

var nanonautX = 50;
var nanonautY = 40;

window.addEventListener('load', start);

function start() {
window.requestAnimationFrame(mainLoop);
}
```

The **MAIN LOOP** section is very short, as we said before:

```
function mainLoop() {
update();
draw();
window.requestAnimationFrame(mainLoop);
}
```

Put this in your **UPDATING** section. We will extend it later:

```
function update() {
}
```

Finally, this goes in your **DRAWING** section:

```
function draw() {
c.clearRect(0, 0, CANVAS_WIDTH, CANVAS_HEIGHT);

// Draw the Nanonaut.
c.drawImage(nanonautImage, nanonautX, nanonautY);
}
```

Now refresh your browser. You should see a Nanonaut floating in the air. Now we have something we can turn into a game!

| Elements | Console | Sources | Network | Timeline | Profiles |

NINJA TIP

The code you'll be using to make your endless runner game is online. You can follow along as we build the game, and copy the code to save time. For more information, go to scholastic.com/coder-dojo/gamecodes

Let's draw some sky in the background and some ground for our Nanonaut to walk on. We want it to look like the image on the left.

So that's basically two rectangles stacked on top of each other. They will cover the entire screen, so replace the `clearRect()` call in the `draw()` function with:

```
function draw() {

// Draw the sky.
c.fillStyle = 'LightSkyBlue';
c.fillRect(0, 0, CANVAS_WIDTH, GROUND_Y - 40);

// Draw the ground.
c.fillStyle = 'ForestGreen';
c.fillRect(0, GROUND_Y - 40, CANVAS_WIDTH, CANVAS_HEIGHT - GROUND_Y + 40);
```

There are four parameters in each set of parentheses that prescribe where each of the rectangles should be drawn. These are the X origin, Y origin, width, and height. The X and Y coordinates originate in the top left of the screen at 0,0. We set up **GROUND_Y** in our constants – it's the ground line that our Nanonaut will run on. This diagram shows the variables that we've used.

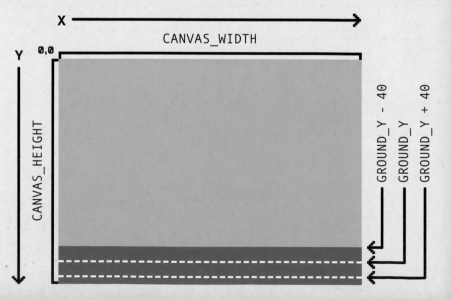

You may have noticed that we're using quite complex color names here, like **LightSkyBlue** and **ForestGreen**. How does the browser know those colors? How can we pick different ones?

Computers are very quick, but not so clever, so we have to tell them exactly what we want. There are lots of different ways to choose colors when working in the browser. The most common ones are specified by name, like we did in the example above, or we can use an **RGB value**.

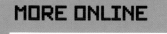

Picking a color by name works because the people making browsers have agreed on a set of color names and exactly which color that is. That's why every browser shows the same color when you ask for **LightSkyBlue** or **BlanchedAlmond**. For once it doesn't matter whether we write **LightSkyBlue** or **lightskyblue** – the browser treats them as the same color.

MORE ONLINE

For a list of colors, visit https://developer.mozilla.org/en-US/docs/Web/CSS/color_value

RGB stands for Red, Green, and Blue. Every color a computer can show is made by mixing these colors together. We can specify a color by telling the computer how much red, green, and blue we want to use. We do that with an RGB value, which is three numbers. Each number states how much of that base color we want, between 0 and 255. Like so:

Red	Green	Blue	Result
255	255	255	**White**
225	0	0	**Red**
0	255	0	**Green**
128	128	0	**Olive**
0	0	0	**Black**

So instead of **ForestGreen** we can write **rgb (34,139,34)**, and instead of **LightSkyBlue** we can use **rgb (135,206,250)**.

THINGS TO DO NEXT

Try playing with the colors. Choose different values and see what colors you can create.

ADDING GRAVITY

Let's put the Nanonaut in their world. In your **SETUP** section, copy the code used to create **nanonautImage**, then amend it to create an image called **backgroundImage** and load a file called **background.png**. Then add this code between the sky and ground lines:

```
c.fillRect(0, 0, CANVAS_WIDTH, GROUND_Y - 40);

// Draw the background.
c.drawImage(backgroundImage, 0, -210);

// Draw the ground.
c.fillStyle = 'ForestGreen';
```

LEVEL UP!

1. We see a Nanonaut in an exciting world.

As you've noticed, our Nanonaut is floating in the sky. And Nanonauts can do a lot of things, but floating is not one of them. What we need to add is **gravity**.

It's always a good idea to start with the basics in game development. We don't need to simulate real gravity, just something that feels and plays nicely. Why don't we just move the Nanonaut down every frame (meaning, every time we update)? Add this at the start of the **update()** function:

```
function update() {
// Update Nanonaut.
nanonautY = nanonautY + 1;
```

The value **1** here is the **speed** by which the Nanonaut falls downward. As you can see, our Nanonaut majestically and slowly ... floats down off the screen. So that's a small improvement, but we don't want the Nanonaut to fall off the screen, and the Nanonaut should fall faster and faster.

Let's look at the first problem. We need to detect when the Nanonaut is on the ground. This is very simple: We just look if the Nanonaut's Y coordinate is higher than the ground, and if so we put them back on the ground. The code looks like this and goes after the code we just added:

```
if (nanonautY > (GROUND_Y - NANONAUT_HEIGHT)) {
nanonautY = GROUND_Y - NANONAUT_HEIGHT;
}
}

// DRAWING
function draw() {
```

This uses an important command: **if**. We use **if** to say "If the **condition** in parentheses is true, execute the **block** of code between the braces." The example below shows the parts of an **if** statement.

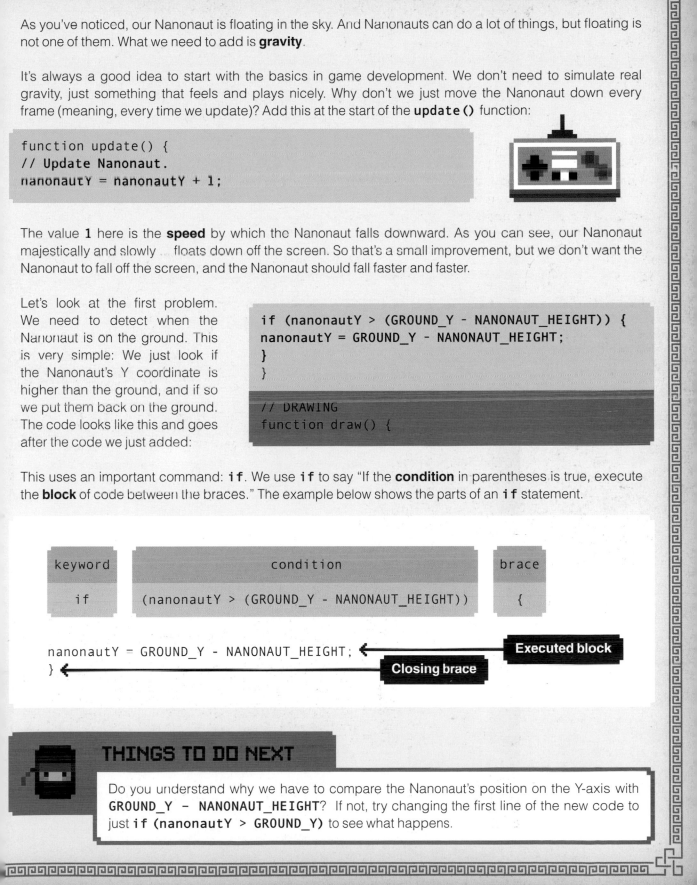

keyword	condition	brace
if	(nanonautY > (GROUND_Y - NANONAUT_HEIGHT))	{

```
nanonautY = GROUND_Y - NANONAUT_HEIGHT;  ← Executed block
}  ← Closing brace
```

THINGS TO DO NEXT

Do you understand why we have to compare the Nanonaut's position on the Y-axis with **GROUND_Y - NANONAUT_HEIGHT**? If not, try changing the first line of the new code to just **if (nanonautY > GROUND_Y)** to see what happens.

Our Nanonaut doesn't fall off the screen anymore, but slowly floating downward is not very realistic. When you drop something in real life, it accelerates. We're going to make our Nanonaut's vertical movement accelerate in our game.

Just as speed works by adding the speed value to the Nanonaut's position every frame, **acceleration** works by adding an acceleration value to the Nanonaut's speed. Acceleration is the speed by which speed changes.

So we'll need some new constants and variables. Add these to the end of the **CONSTANTS** and **SETUP** sections:

```
var NANONAUT_Y_ACCELERATION = 1;
```

```
var nanonautYSpeed = 0;
```

And change the **update()** function like so:

```
nanonautY = nanonautY + nanonautYSpeed;
nanonautYSpeed = nanonautYSpeed + NANONAUT_Y_ACCELERATION;
if (nanonautY > (GROUND_Y - NANONAUT_HEIGHT)) {
nanonautY = GROUND_Y - NANONAUT_HEIGHT;
nanonautYSpeed = 0;
}
```

Refresh the page and the Nanonaut should fall toward the ground faster and faster.

LEVEL UP!

2. The Nanonaut will fall to the ground.

HANDLING INPUT

Now we want to be able to make the Nanonaut jump. First, let's see how we can react to player input. Our game will be controlled with the keyboard, so we need to find out which key the player is pressing. Then, when the player presses the correct key, the Nanonaut will jump.

We can find out what is happening with the keyboard using the browser API. Remember how we got the browser to call us when it was done loading? That was just one event: **load**. There are a lot more. The ones we're interested in are called **keydown** and **keyup**. Whenever the player presses a key down or releases a key, these events will be triggered, and any callbacks will be called.

At the end of the **SETUP** section, before adding the **load** event listener, add:

```
window.addEventListener('keydown', onKeyDown);

window.addEventListener('load', start);
```

This is similar to what we saw on page 26. Whenever the player presses a key, the **keydown** event is triggered, and here we're saying we want it to call a function named **onKeyDown** whenever that happens.

```
function onKeyDown(event) {
console.log(event.keyCode);
}
```

onKeyDown is a function that expects an **event** parameter. This parameter is an object from the browser, containing everything we need to know about the triggered event. In this case, the object can tell us what happened to the keyboard, so we access the **keyCode** property to find out which key was pressed.

Add this code to **PLAYER INPUT**, then run the program and press keys. What appears in the console?

NINJA TIP

Different event types are sent different event objects. Mouse events, which we don't cover in this book, get events with information about where the mouse is, for instance. The **load** event, which we saw earlier, doesn't get any information at all! It's enough to know that everything is loaded.

CONDITIONS AND VARIABLES

Refresh and press some keys, and you'll see that each key shows a different number in the console. This is the key's **code**. We are interested in the space key, which has a key code of 32.

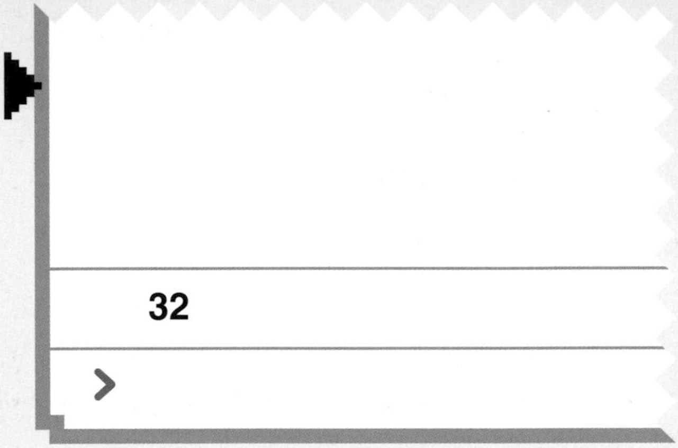

To see if the space key is pressed, we replace the **console.log** line inside **onKeyDown()** with these three lines:

```
function onKeyDown(event) {
if (event.keyCode === 32) {
console.log("Space key pressed");
}
```

In this case the condition for the **if** statement is **event.keyCode === 32**, which means "if the **keyCode** property of the object named **event** is equal to 32." We use three equal signs in JavaScript because we want to be really, really, really sure the two sides are equal.

32

>

NINJA TIP

Never use one equal sign in a condition, such as "if (x = 5)". The computer won't complain, but it won't do what you expect.

42

We know how to check whether the space key is pressed, but what do we want to do with that? For now, we just want to store whether the key is pressed, nothing more. So we need to put that in a variable somehow.

We also said we don't want to use magic numbers like 32! So we need to replace that with a constant that has a clear name.

In your **CONSTANTS** section, add:

```
var SPACE_KEYCODE = 32;
```

We saw that a variable can be a number, or a string. It can also be a **boolean**, named after the mathematician George Boole. A boolean can have one of two values: **true** or **false**. This is ideal for our purposes.

In **SETUP**, after **nanonautYSpeed**, add:

```
var spaceKeyIsPressed = false;
```

And replace the body of **onKeyDown** with:

```
if (event.keyCode === SPACE_KEYCODE) {
spaceKeyIsPressed = true;
}
```

JUMPING

So we know when the space key is pressed down, but we also need to detect when it's released too. Luckily, that's pretty straightforward.

In your **SETUP** section, after the line for the **keydown** handler, add:

```
window.addEventListener('keydown', onKeyDown);
window.addEventListener('keyup', onKeyUp);
```

After the **onKeyDown** function, add this:

```
spaceKeyIsPressed = true;
}
}
function onKeyUp(event) {
if (event.keyCode === SPACE_KEYCODE) {
spaceKeyIsPressed = false;
}
}
```

As you can see, it's the same as it is for the **keydown** event, only opposite.

Now, how do we actually jump? We have gravity pulling the Nanonaut down, decreasing their vertical speed, so we need something else to increase their vertical speed. Add this to your **CONSTANTS**:

```
var NANONAUT_JUMP_SPEED = 20;
```

Then add this at the start of the **update()** function:

```
function update() {
if (spaceKeyIsPressed) {
nanonautYSpeed = -NANONAUT_JUMP_SPEED;
}
```

Try pressing the space bar now. When you keep the space key pressed, the Nanonaut flies off into space! No matter how cool Nanonauts are, they can't fly.

This happens because the Nanonaut can jump while in the air, so we need to detect and forbid that. Can you figure out how?

We're going to introduce another boolean variable called **nanonautIsInTheAir**, which will be **true** when the Nanonaut is in the air. This will be a global variable, so add it to your **SETUP** section:

```
var nanonautYSpeed = 0;
var nanonautIsInTheAir = false;
```

At the start, the variable will be **false**. When the player presses the space key, we'll set it to **true**.

How do we know the Nanonaut is back on the ground? Remember the check to stop the Nanonaut from falling out of the world? That's how. So, in **update()** we need to add new parts to two functions:

```
if (spaceKeyIsPressed && !nanonautIsInTheAir) {
nanonautYSpeed = -NANONAUT_JUMP_SPEED;
nanonautIsInTheAir = true;
}
```

```
if (nanonautY > (GROUND_Y - NANONAUT_HEIGHT)) {
nanonautY = GROUND_Y - NANONAUT_HEIGHT;
nanonautYSpeed = 0;
nanonautIsInTheAir = false;
}
```

Let's look at that first if statement. We need to check if the player pressed the space key and if the Nanonaut is in the air. The Nanonaut can only jump when not in the air, so we use **!**, the **logical not operator**, on **nanonautIsInTheAir**. And then we use the **logical and operator**, which is written as **&&**, to make sure the if block is only executed when both conditions are true.

LEVEL UP!

3. The Nanonaut can jump into the air.

ADDING MOVEMENT

Now our Nanonaut needs to move. Add this to your **CONSTANTS** section:

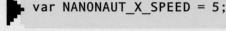

```
var NANONAUT_X_SPEED = 5;
```

And at the start of **update()**, add:

```
function update() {
  nanonautX = nanonautX + NANONAUT_X_SPEED;
```

Try it out. What do you see? That's right: Our Nanonaut runs off-screen, never to be seen again. We need to make a **camera** that follows the Nanonaut. The world will be bigger than the screen, and the screen will only show what our "camera" sees. We call what the camera sees the **viewport**. As the Nanonaut and the camera move to the right through the world, the world will appear to move left. This is called **scrolling**.

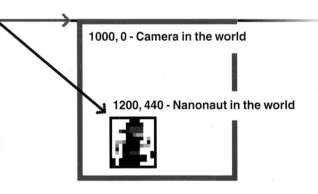

To do this is not very difficult. Imagine the Nanonaut has these coordinates:

0,0

1000, 0 - Camera in the world

1200, 440 - Nanonaut in the world

And then we calculate where that object would be relative to the viewport. To do that, we just subtract the coordinates of the camera in the world from the coordinates of the Nanonaut in the world:

0,0

200, 440 - Nanonaut relative to camera

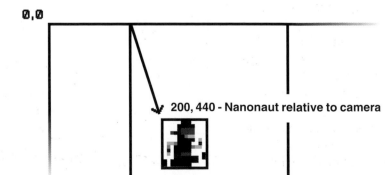

We call this going from **world space**, where coordinates of things are relative to the origin of the world, to **screen space**, where coordinates are relative to the origin of the canvas. And the operation we're using is called a **transformation**.

How do we do this in our game? First, add some variables to your **SETUP** code called **cameraX** and **cameraY**. Assign them **0** at first.

Then, for everything that we want to move when the camera moves, we need to add the transformation in our **DRAWING** code. Replace the old **drawImage** call, which we use to draw the Nanonaut, with:

```
c.drawImage(nanonautImage, nanonautX - cameraX, nanonautY - cameraY);
```

OK, try it out! You should see ... no difference. Why? Because we're not moving the camera. Add this to the end of your **update()** function:

```
nanonautIsInTheAir = false;
}

// Update camera
cameraX = nanonautX - 150;
}
```

This line says: Place the camera so that it shows 150 pixels to the left of the Nanonaut.

Try it out. Now we're back where we started. The Nanonaut jumps in one place. Why can't we see them move forward? We're not moving the background! The camera and the Nanonaut are both moving through the world, but it's invisible to us. What if we used this to draw the background?

```
c.drawImage(backgroundImage, 0 - cameraX, -210);
```

Now the background will move ... but it moves off-screen and never comes back! We need to repeat the background. How do we do that? Do we just add dozens of **drawImage** calls to repeat the image indefinitely and create a longer background? That seems like a waste because most of them would be off-screen at any point.

In fact, we only ever need to see two background images. Let's add this to our **CONSTANTS**:

```
var BACKGROUND_WIDTH = 1000;
```

And change the background drawing code inside your **draw()** function to this:

```
// Draw the background.
var backgroundX = - (cameraX % BACKGROUND_WIDTH);
c.drawImage(backgroundImage, backgroundX, -210);
```

Try it out. We're nearly there! So what does the line that calculates **backgroundX** do?

First of all, as you can see, we can just write "- something" instead of "0 - something".

Second, we're using the percent sign. This is called the **modulo operator**. An operator is something like plus or minus that operates on a value, and modulo is just the remainder of a division. So we're saying "Give us the remainder of the camera's X coordinate divided by the background width." Because we don't care which "copy" of the background it is: We just care about placing it relative to the camera.

And how do we close the gap? Simple: Just draw the background a second time:

```
c.drawImage(backgroundImage, backgroundX, -210);
c.drawImage(backgroundImage, backgroundX + BACKGROUND_WIDTH, -210);
```

There's still a little flash of blue at the start of the game. That's because the start position of the Nanonaut isn't quite right. Change this in the **SETUP** section:

```
var nanonautX = CANVAS_WIDTH / 2;
var nanonautY = GROUND_Y - NANONAUT_HEIGHT;
```

Now the Nanonaut doesn't drop out of the sky anymore, and the flash of blue is gone. And the scrolling works!

LEVEL UP!

> 4. The Nanonaut automatically runs to the right, followed by the camera.

There's something important going on in the code we just wrote. Did you notice how we're using **var** to declare variables? But these are not in our **SETUP** or **CONSTANTS** sections, they're inside a function. Variables like that are called **local variables**, because they can only be used locally, inside the function where they are declared.

This means only code inside the **draw()** function can use the **backgroundX** variable. All the other variables we've been using so far are not inside functions or other code blocks. They are at the top level of the program. This makes them **global variables**.

When you refer to a variable, JavaScript first looks for a variable in the current function, then among the global variables. This means it's very important to make sure your local variables have different names to global variables. What do you think you'd see if you were to run this code:

```
var myBeautifulCounter = 0;

function doSomethingImportant() {
var myBeautifulCounter = 1;
console.log(myBeautifulCounter);
}
```

That's right: 1, because the browser uses the local variable, not the global one.

This kind of thing can lead to hard-to-find bugs. Some people give special names to global variables, or try to avoid them altogether. But in this book we just try to be careful, because using global variables makes things easier to explain.

SPRITESHEETS

Our Nanonaut glides across the screen. Wouldn't it look better if the Nanonaut was running? We need **animation**. As we saw before, animation works by quickly showing different images. So to have our Nanonaut run, we need to show different images.

Now, we could load multiple images and draw them over and over again in sequence. But there's an easier way: **spritesheets**. A **sprite** is an image, like the one we're using for the Nanonaut. A spritesheet is multiple images stuck together. If we can tell the browser to just draw a part of that image, we can animate simply by picking different parts.

This is a very common technique in 2D games. The graphics package we prepared has a spritesheet we made already. If you want to use your own graphics, have a look at page 93 to see what it should look like. In any case, make sure it's in your **nanonauts** folder, just like the other images.

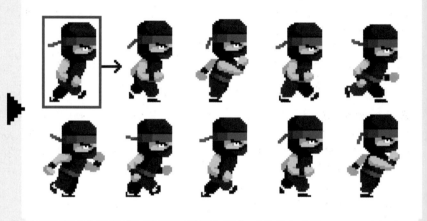

Before we continue programming, let's think about what we need to do next.

We need to load **animatedNanonaut.png** instead of **nanonaut.png**. That is the easiest thing to do. In your program, just change the file name of your **Image()** to **animatedNanonaut.png**.

We need to tell the browser to draw part of an image, or things will look very strange. Try it now!

There is a second version of **drawImage()**, the API function we're using in the **draw()** function to draw our Nanonaut. This version takes different parameters. We can tell it exactly which rectangle to take from the image and which rectangle to draw it in on the canvas.

We need to switch from one Nanonaut image, or **animation frame**, to the next. But this is trickier than it looks.

We probably don't want to switch the image every frame, because it will be too fast. So we need to count each time we go through our main loop before we decide to switch to the next image.

Finally, picking the next image is not super-easy. We need to move along each row until we get to the end, then move back to the start but one row down, unless it's the last row, because then we go back to the top left. Yikes!

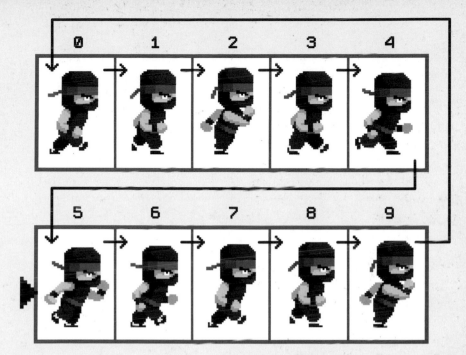

But maybe we can look at the problem differently. If we give every frame a number, and we write code that gives us the coordinate for each number, we don't need to do any complicated "should we move down a row" logic. We just increase the number, and find out where that frame is. That is much easier than keeping X and Y coordinates and updating those.

First we need some constants:

```
var NANONAUT_NR_FRAMES_PER_ROW = 5;
var NANONAUT_NR_ANIMATION_FRAMES = 7;
```

Then we need a variable to store the current frame number. Add this line to the other global variable declarations in the **SETUP** section:

```
var spaceKeyIsPressed = false;
var nanonautFrameNr = 0;
```

The frame number is set to zero because computers start counting at zero. Now we need to calculate the row and column in our spritesheet from the frame number and turn those into coordinates in pixels. For that we'll need some basic math.

To find the row, if we just divide the frame number by 5, which is the number of frames per row, we will get:

0	0.2	0.4	0.6	0.8
1	1.2	1.4	1.6	1.8

DRAWING SPRITES

That's not quite what we want. Frame 7 is in row 1, not row 1.4. So we need to throw away everything after the decimal point. In JavaScript we use a function called **Math.floor()**. **Math** is an object with lots of handy mathematical functions in it, and **floor()** rounds the number down.

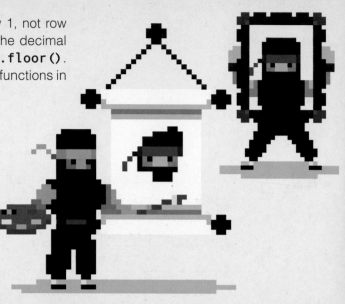

To get the column, we need the reverse – we need to get the remainder of dividing the frame number by 5. As we saw on page 48, we can use the modulo operator to calculate the remainder. Once we have the row and column, all we need to do is multiply it with **NANONAUT_WIDTH** and **NANONAUT_HEIGHT** to get the coordinates in pixels.

Now to draw the sprite! Replace the Nanonaut **drawImage()** line with:

```
// Draw the Nanonaut.
var nanonautSpriteSheetRow = Math.floor(nanonautFrameNr /
NANONAUT_NR_FRAMES_PER_ROW);
var nanonautSpriteSheetColumn = nanonautFrameNr % NANONAUT_NR_FRAMES_PER_ROW;
var nanonautSpriteSheetX = nanonautSpriteSheetColumn * NANONAUT_WIDTH;
var nanonautSpriteSheetY = nanonautSpriteSheetRow * NANONAUT_HEIGHT;
c.drawImage(nanonautImage, nanonautSpriteSheetX, nanonautSpriteSheetY,
NANONAUT_WIDTH, NANONAUT_HEIGHT, nanonautX - cameraX, nanonautY - cameraY,
NANONAUT_WIDTH, NANONAUT_HEIGHT);
}
```

The new **drawImage()** call takes the following parameters:

- ☻ The image to draw from.

- ☻ The X and Y coordinates of the rectangle from the image to take.

- ☻ How wide and how high that rectangle is.

- ☻ The X and Y coordinates where the part from the image should be drawn.

- ☻ How wide and how high that part should be.

At the end of **update ()**, before the line where we set the camera position, add:

```
//Update Animation
nanonautFrameNr = nanonautFrameNr + 1;
if (nanonautFrameNr >= NANONAUT_NR_ANIMATION_FRAMES) {
nanonautFrameNr = 0;
}

// Update camera.
```

NINJA TIP

These are some common mathematical operators used in JavaScript.

COMPARISON OPERATORS		
>	Greater than	5 is greater than 3 (e.g., 5 > 3)
<	Less than	3 is less than 5 (3 < 5)
===	Equal to	2 is equal to 2 (2 === 2)
!==	Not equal to	2 is not equal to 4 (2 !== 4)
>=	Greater than or equal	2 is greater than or equal to 2 (2 >= 2)
<=	Less than or equal	1 is less than or equal to 2 (1 <= 2)

Refresh the browser and you should see a running Nanonaut.

Only ... a Nanonaut that is running much too fast. To solve the animation speed problem, we want to make sure we don't increase the Nanonaut animation frame every game frame, meaning every time we go through the main loop. So we want to say something like "Every three game frames, add one to the Nanonaut animation frame." Now we *could* do this:

```
nanonautAnimationCounter = nanonautAnimationCounter + 1;
if (nanonautAnimationCounter >= 3) {
nanonautFrameNr = nanonautFrameNr + 1;
if (nanonautFrameNr >= NANONAUT_NR_ANIMATION_FRAMES) {
nanonautFrameNr = 0;
}
nanonautAnimationCounter = 0;
}
```

But that's another variable to keep track of. For every animated thing we add, we'll need another variable. Is there an easier way to go "every third frame"? It turns out there is, and we saw it earlier: the modulo operator.

Let's start with a new constant:

```
var NANONAUT_ANIMATION_SPEED = 3;
```

Then add a variable that counts game frames to the other global variable declarations in our **SETUP** section:

```
var gameFrameCounter = 0;
```

And then at the start of **update()** we add one to this new variable:

```
function update() {
gameFrameCounter = gameFrameCounter + 1;
```

And finally we replace the update animation code at the end of **update()** with:

```
if ((gameFrameCounter % NANONAUT_ANIMATION_SPEED) === 0) {
nanonautFrameNr = nanonautFrameNr + 1;
if (nanonautFrameNr >= NANONAUT_NR_ANIMATION_FRAMES) {
nanonautFrameNr = 0;
}
}
```

Do you see what the modulo operator is doing? It gives us the remainder of dividing the counter by **NANONAUT_ANIMATION_SPEED**. That remainder is only zero every third frame.

LEVEL UP!

5. The Nanonaut is animated.

Now that our Nanonaut character is animated, try lowering the value of **NANONAUT_ANIMATION_SPEED** to see the Nanonaut move in slow-motion.

NINJA TIP

Computers follow rules of precedence that dictate which elements are evaluated first. Addition and subtraction have a low precedence, while parentheses have a high precedence. In our example, we use brackets so the computer calculates the remainder first, then compares it to 0.

What now? How about we make the world more interesting with background elements?

Create an image in the **SETUP** section named **bush1Image** and load **bush1.png**. Then draw it at the X coordinate of 550, and Y coordinate of **GROUND_Y - 100**.

NINJA TIP

If you find creating this image difficult, look back at how we set up the Nanonaut image on page 34.

Then draw the image again at the X coordinate of 750, and the Y coordinate of **GROUND_Y - 90**.

The screen should look like this:

Although we only added two **drawImage** calls, you can imagine that we are going to need more, to make this seem lively. And, of course, we'll have to deal with the bushes scrolling off-screen again! But we'll come to that later.

Adding all those calls will become annoying, as we keep repeating lines of code with only small differences. If we ever want to have those bushes come from a spritesheet, we'd have to change a lot of calls, and we could make a mistake anywhere.

ARRAYS

Whenever you come across repetitive code, like the parameters for drawing the bush, it's worth thinking about whether we can make the computer do more work for us. Of course we can! But we need to learn about a couple of useful new features. First: **arrays**.

Arrays are simply lists of values or variables. They're written like this:

```
var myThings = [12, 93, 72];
```

Everything between the square brackets, separated by commas, goes into the array. So the variable **myThings** is an array that contains three elements: the number **12**, the number **93**, and the number **72**.

You can put any kind of value in an array, and variables too!

```
var stuff = [17, 'hello', true];
```

The variable **stuff** contains three elements: the number **17**, the string **hello**, and a boolean value of **true**.

Each element of the array has a number, which starts at 0. This number is called the **index**.

```
var myThings = [12, 93, 72];
```

You use the index to get a value out of an array. For example, to print the second element of **myThings** to the console, you'd write:

```
console.log(myThings[1]);
```

That would print the number 93. See how you need to use the index **1** to get the second element? Before we look at what we use arrays for, let's look at another new concept: the **for** command. Often when we program we want to have **loops**, which repeats code a certain number of times, or while some condition is true. Until now, when we wanted something done twice, we just repeated the code, like we did here:

```
c.drawImage(bush1Image, 550, GROUND_Y - 100);
c.drawImage(bush1Image, 750, GROUND_Y - 90);
```

But what if we don't know yet how many times we want to do something? What if it comes from a variable? What if we don't want to write, and change, the same line 100 times?

We've already seen on page 16 that you can type directly into the console to test a line of code. You can also do this with longer blocks of code like **for** loops! Type this into the console:

```
for (var i=0; i<5; i++) {
console.log(i);
}
```

0
1
2
3
4

> for (var i=0; i<5; i++) { console.log(i); }

You will see the numbers 0 to 4 appear. The computer executed the **console.log()** line five times, and added one to a variable each time. How?

The **for** command consists of four parts:

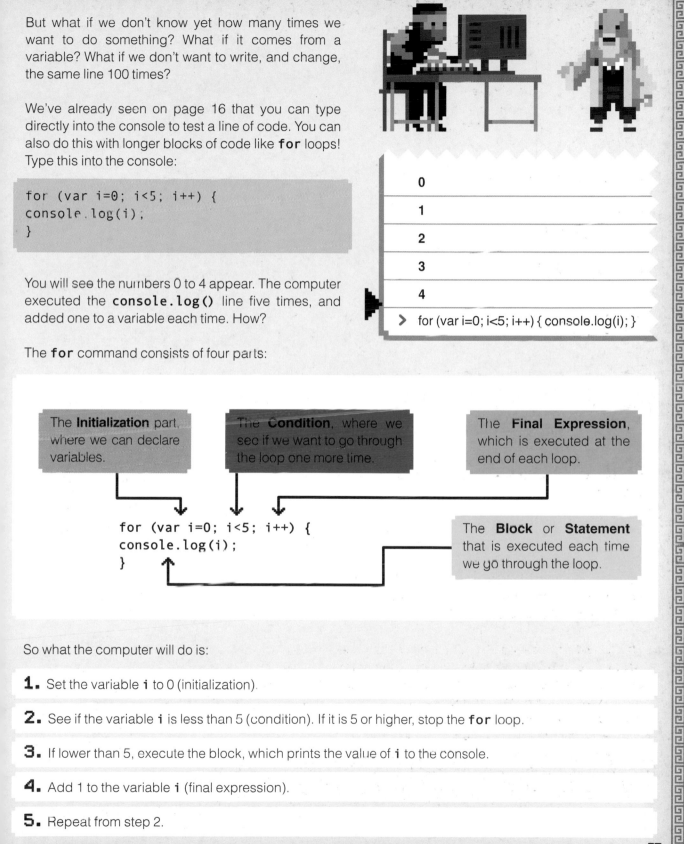

The **Initialization** part, where we can declare variables.

The **Condition**, where we see if we want to go through the loop one more time.

The **Final Expression**, which is executed at the end of each loop.

```
for (var i=0; i<5; i++) {
console.log(i);
}
```

The **Block** or **Statement** that is executed each time we go through the loop.

So what the computer will do is:

1. Set the variable **i** to 0 (initialization).

2. See if the variable **i** is less than 5 (condition). If it is 5 or higher, stop the **for** loop.

3. If lower than 5, execute the block, which prints the value of **i** to the console.

4. Add 1 to the variable **i** (final expression).

5. Repeat from step 2.

FOR LOOPS

There are many things you can do with for loops, and there are other, more advanced loops as well. But this one, where we just do something a certain number of times, can be used for lots of things.

What does this have to do with arrays? Well, if we want to do something with what's in an array, we need to look at each element in turn. And that means we need a loop.

Type this into the console of your browser:

```
var myArray = [7, 19, 23];
for (var i=0; i<3; i++) {
console.log(myArray[i]);
}
```

You will see the numbers 7, 19, and 23 appear. The computer looped like before, except instead of printing the **i** variable, we used **i** as the index to the array and printed the first element (element 0), then the second, then the third.

7
19
23

> var myArray = [7, 19, 23]; for (var i=0; i<3; i++) { console.log(myArray[i]); }

But what if our array grows longer? We don't want to have to change the for statement every time. Can we ask the array how many elements it has? Yes, we can:

```
var myArray = [7, 19, 23, 2];
for (var i=0; i<myArray.length; i++) {
console.log(myArray[i]);
}
```

`myArray.length` always equals the number of elements in the array.

NINJA TIP

Didn't we say variables should have memorable names? Then why use **i**? Well, the **i** variable is only used as an index inside the loop and has no other meaning. It's acceptable to use very short variable names in cases like this instead of, say, `arrayElementIndex`.

So now we can improve our bush-drawing code! In your **SETUP** section, add the line to the other global variable declarations:

```
var bushXCoordinates = [ 550, 750, 1000, 1200 ];
```

In your `draw()` function, change the two bush-drawing lines to:

```
for (var i=0; i<bushXCoordinates.length; i++) {
c.drawImage(bush1Image, bushXCoordinates[i] - cameraX, GROUND_Y - 100 -
cameraY);
}
```

Now run it! It should look like this image on the left.

We have lots of bushes in the background, and if we want to change them, or add more, we just need to change the array.

What if we want to change the Y coordinate for each bush as well?

| Elements | Console | Sources | Network | Timeline | Profiles |

BETTER BUSH DRAWING

Our first attempt might be to write:

```
var bushYCoordinates = [ 100, 80, 90, 85 ];

for (var i=0; i<bushXCoordinates.length; i++) {
c.drawImage(bush1Image, bushXCoordinates[i] -
cameraX, GROUND_Y - bushYCoordinates[i] -cameraY);
}
```

That would work, but it doesn't feel right. What if the two arrays don't have the same length? That feels like a bug waiting to happen, and because good programmers know they're not perfect, they like to use **defensive programming** to make bugs less likely.

But there's another reason why it doesn't feel right. The X and Y coordinates of a bush belong together, so why are they spread out over two different arrays?

And what will happen if we want to have different kinds of bushes? Do we need a third array that says what kind of bush this is?

It's time to revisit **objects**. We had a look at them back on page 21, and we've been using objects from the browser API, such as **document**, **event**, and **console**.

Objects are a way to bundle values that belong together. This is another way to draw our bush, for instance:

```
var aBush = { x: 50, y: 100 };
c.drawImage(bush1Image, aBush.x - cameraX,
GROUND_Y - aBush.y - cameraY);
```

Let's have a closer look at that first line, and let's write it a bit differently so it's clearer:

```
var aBush = {
x: 50,
y: 100
};
```

The computer will still understand this. It doesn't care if we go to a new line, it only looks for the closing brace and the semicolon.

We're declaring a variable called **aBush**, and the value is this thing in braces. When we use braces like this, it means we're defining an object. Here we're saying "Create a fresh object, and give it a property with the name **x** and the value **50**, and another property with the name **y** and the value **100**."

We can get the value of a property using the dot operator, as we've seen before:

```
console.log(aBush.x);
```

50

>

This would print 50 in the console.

Property names can be any string. But that leads to a problem. What if we want to name a property "hey you"? This won't work;

```
var myDifficultObject = {
hey you: 20
};
```

The computer doesn't like the space in the property name.

Try it! The browser will complain, saying there's a **syntax error**, because it doesn't understand what we want.

! **SyntaxError: undefined**

>

For this case, there is another way to define and retrieve properties:

```
var myDifficultObject = {
"hey you": 20
};
console.log(myDifficultObject["hey you"]);
```

It does the same thing but uses quote marks, which works for almost any property name.

20

>

USING THE OBJECTS

Once you've created an object, you can change it. For instance, you can change the property value of an object by stating:

```
aBush.x = 23;
```

Or you can add a property to the object:

```
aBush.hasBirdsInIt = true;
```

When you ask for a property that doesn't exist, you will get back a special value called "undefined."

```
console.log(aBush.likesToDance);
```

This example will print "undefined" in the console, because we never specified whether bushes like to dance (they don't).

> **! undefined**
>
> **> console.log(aBush.likesToDance);**

Just like with arrays, the values of properties can have any type. This works fine:

```
var importantData = {
age: 17,
favoriteSaying: "hello",
canProgram: true
};
```

In fact, this works too:

```
var aPerson = {
position: { x: 50, y: 100 },
name: "Sam",
luckyNumbers: [7, 22]
};
```

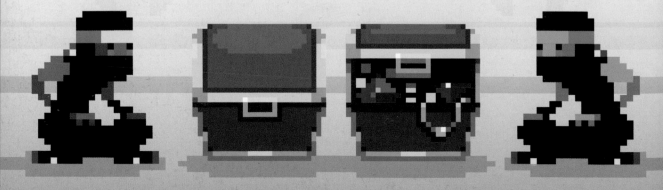

You can put arrays and objects inside other arrays and objects. This allows you to create complex data structures, which can be useful.

And can we make arrays of objects? Yes! Let's do that for our bushes.

First, create a second bush image called **bush2Image** in the **SETUP** section, and make it load **bush2.png**.

Then, replace the bush data you had ...

```
var bushXCoordinates = [ 550, 750, 1000, 1200 ];
```

... with this new code:

```
var bushData = [{
x: 550,
y: 100,
image: bush1Image
}, {
x: 750,
y: 90,
image: bush2Image
}];
```

If you want to add more bushes, you can add more objects. Now we need to change our bush-drawing loop. First of all, make the for command use **bushData**, not **bushXCoordinates**.

We saw that we can get the second element from an array with: `myArray[i]`

And we can get a property from an object with: `myObject.x`

We can combine that to: `myArray[i].x`

Replace the bush-drawing loop inside your **draw()** function with:

```
// Draw the bushes.
for (var i=0; i<bushData.length; i++) {
c.drawImage(bushData[i].image, bushData[i].x -
cameraX, GROUND_Y - bushData[i].y - cameraY);
}
```

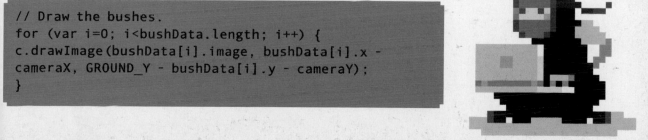

UPDATING THE BUSHES

That's better. Except the bushes scroll off-screen and then they're gone forever. We had the same problem with the background. This time we're going to solve it slightly differently. We want to look for any bushes that have gone off-screen on the left, and then increase their X coordinate so they'll come back in from the right.

Add this to the end of your **update()** function:

```
// Update bushes.
for (var i=0; i<bushData.length; i++) {
if ((bushData[i].x - cameraX) < -CANVAS_WIDTH) {
bushData[i].x += (2 * CANVAS_WIDTH) + 150;
}
}
}
```

Let's look at the new code in more detail. First, we loop over all the bushes:

```
for (var i=0; i<bushData.length; i++) {
```

Then for each bush, we see if it's off-screen relative to the camera:

```
if ((bushData[i].x - cameraX) < -CANVAS_WIDTH) {
```

Comparing it to **CANVAS_WIDTH** is overly generous – we can be very sure the bush is off-screen by the time this condition becomes true – but this way the code works even if we add very big bushes.

Finally, if the bush is off-screen, we add a number to its X coordinate to move it to the right of the camera again:

```
bushData[i].x += (2 * CANVAS_WIDTH) + 150;
```

Try it. The bushes will keep coming back.

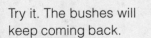

That's cool ... except the bushes are not spread out very nicely. We could add more bushes to **bushData**, but can't we get the computer to do this for us? Yes we can! If you look at the bush data we have so far, you'll see it's quite predictable. So we can probably use the computer to generate that data.

Whenever you have a nice, clear thing you want the computer to do, it's a good idea to put it in a function. That way it's off in a corner, we know it works, and the code that calls the function becomes simpler. We definitely want to use a function to generate bushes. Start with replacing the **bushData** variable inside your **SETUP** code:

```
var bushData = [{
x: 550,
y: 100,
image: bush1Image
}, {
x: 750,
y: 90,
image: bush2Image
}];
```

with this:

```
var bushData = generateBushes();
```

And after the **start** function, at the end of **SETUP**, write:

```
function generateBushes() {
var generatedBushData = [];
return generatedBushData;
}
```

The **return** command allows us to return a value from a function. The local array **generatedBushData** will be assigned to the variable **bushData**.

This function doesn't do anything useful yet, but it does run without any errors. When you're making big changes and breaking stuff, it's good to always make sure your program runs. That way you don't have to remember where all the broken things are.

NINJA TIP

When you know something is wrong in your program but it's not the right time to fix it, you can add comments to yourself, like this:
```
// TO DO: Fix - the code doesn't do anything yet!
```
That helps you remember later what you need to do.

RANDOM NUMBERS

We want to spread the bushes out horizontally and vertically, and we want it to look irregular. To create irregularity, we need **random numbers**. Just as you can't predict whether a tossed coin will be heads or tails, you can't predict random numbers. We can get JavaScript to generate them for us by calling the API function `Math.random()`.

Type the following in the console of your browser:

```
for (var i=0; i<10; i++) { console.log(Math.random()); }
```

0.7315165467698956

0.43915116187796366

0.123328522528195629

0.18729668080235085

0.04714256657847582

0.8676065784271989

0.6399414110144506

0.29280905124004597

0.8895071785872819

0.45679113256276816

>

You will see 10 very long numbers, all between 0 and 1. In fact, these numbers are guaranteed to be greater than 0, and smaller than 1. Also, they don't follow a regular pattern.

The direct output of `Math.random()` is useless, because their range is so small. To make them useful, we need to multiply them with a number, so that they spread out over a longer range.

Put this code in the `generateBushes()` function:

```
var generatedBushData = [];
generatedBushData.push({
x: 550,
y: 80 + Math.random() * 20,
image: bush1Image
});
return generatedBushData;
}
```

We create a new object, with a fixed X coordinate, a Y coordinate that lies at a random point in a range between 80 and 100, and a fixed image. Then we use **push** to add that object to the end of the bush array.

When you refresh the game lots of times, you will see that the bush is positioned at slightly different coordinates.

So, can we do the same for the X coordinate? Let's try by making the following change:

```
generatedBushData.push({
x: 550 + Math.random() * CANVAS_WIDTH,
y: 80 + Math.random() * 20,
```

What's with the magic numbers in this function? Didn't we say those should go into **CONSTANTS**? Yes, but for a reason that doesn't apply here. We know that each of these numbers will only be used once, and always inside this function. They're the function's secrets, so it's fine.

OK, that one bush has a random X coordinate now. Let's try generating 10 of them by putting this for loop around the push call:

```
var generatedBushData = [];
for (var i=0; i<10; i++) {
generatedBushData.push({
x: 550 + Math.random() * CANVAS_WIDTH,
y: 80 + Math.random() * 20,
image: bush1Image
});
}
return generatedBushData;
```

Catastrophe! The bushes are too close together, and sometimes they overlap in ugly ways. We're using the bushes' Y coordinates to create a false sense of depth, making the scene feel more three-dimensional. But this only works when we never draw a higher bush over a lower bush.

So how do we solve this? Instead of calculating a random X coordinate for each bush, we're going to calculate random gap widths between the bushes. That way we can be sure they never overlap.

Make the following changes:

```
function generateBushes() {
var generatedBushData = [];
var bushX = 0;
for (var i=0; i<10; i++) {
generatedBushData.push({
x: bushX,
y: 80 + Math.random() * 20,
image: bush1Image
});
bushX += 150 + Math.random() * 200;
```

Try that. You can see most of the bushes don't overlap anymore. Most ... but not all. We still get some clumps in one place. Why? Because we're generating too many bushes. As you can see from the code we wrote earlier, the bushes get pushed back **2 * CANVAS_WIDTH** pixels. We're probably generating more than that.

There are two ways to solve this: Either we store how wide all of the bushes we generated are, and push them back by that amount. Or we generate just enough bushes. Let's try the latter solution.

THE WHILE COMMAND

We want to go "While the X coordinate is less than **2 * CANVAS_WIDTH**, go through this loop." It turns out there's a way to say exactly that in JavaScript using the **while** command, which works like this:

```
while (condition) {
...this is executed as long as the condition is true...
}
```

In our case, that means this ...

```
var bushX = 0;
for (var i=0; i<10; i++) {
```

... becomes:

```
var bushX = 0;
while (bushX < (2 * CANVAS_WIDTH)) {
```

Now for the final touch of randomly picking a bush image. We know **Math.random** returns a number between 0 and 1, so we have a 50% chance of that number being greater or equal to 0.5. So we can just do this:

Now refresh your game a couple of times. You'll see that sometimes it loads **bush1Image**, and other times it will load **bush2Image**.

As you can see, the if statement has a trick up its sleeve: the **else clause**. We can write:

```
while (bushX < (2 * CANVAS_WIDTH)) {
var bushImage;
if (Math.random() >= 0.5) {
bushImage = bush1Image;
} else {
bushImage = bush2Image;
}
generatedBushData.push({
x: bushX,
y: 80 + Math.random() * 20,
image: bushImage
});
```

```
if (condition) {
...this is executed if the condition is true...
} else {
...this is executed if the condition is NOT true...
}
```

Everything in the second code block, after the **else** keyword, is only executed when the if statement's condition is not true. That's exactly what we want here!

LEVEL UP!

6. There are background objects to make the world more lively.

OVERLOADING FUNCTIONS

Next on our to-do list: "Evil animated robots running from right to left." That should be easy, right? We've already animated the Nanonaut, so it's just the same code.

But wait a minute. Are we saying we're going to duplicate code? Is that what we want? Or do we want to take the code we have and make it work for both Nanonauts and robots?

This is a decision you have to make very often when programming. Most of the time you don't want to write the same code twice, because it takes up more space, it's harder to change, and it's more likely to contain mistakes. But sometimes if you take two things that are almost the same, and write one piece of code that handles both, you can end up with something quite ugly.

If you had a function to make omelets and one for pancakes, you might go "Hey, those are similar! I can do that with one function." And then before you know it, you end up with:

```
function make_pancake_or_omelet(batter, filling_if_omelet, is_pancake) {
// Stir batter...

if (!is_pancake) {
pan.put(filling_if_omelet);
}

// Flip if pancake, fold if omelet

if (is_pancake) {
pan.pour(syrup);
}
}
```

It turns out pancakes and omelets aren't that similar! There's lots of special case logic inside this function. There are parameters that only make sense for omelets, not pancakes! The same can apply to code as well – the more special cases there are, the more chance your code will become a mess.

In our case, animating a Nanonaut is quite like animating a robot. So we can try to do both in one function.

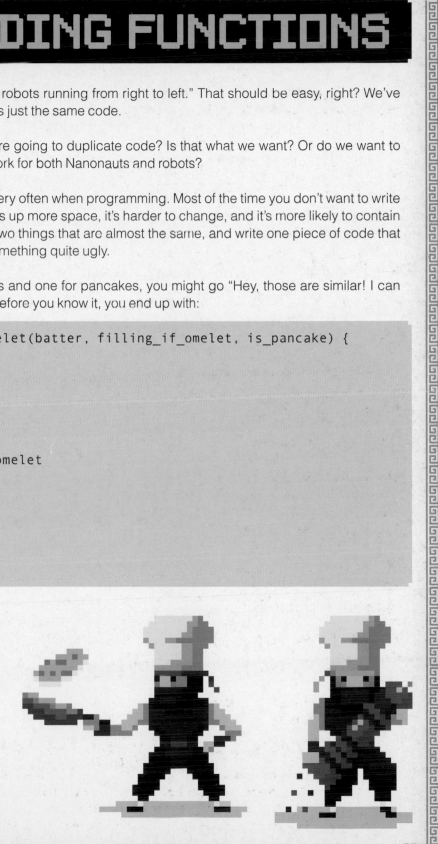

MULTITASKING FUNCTIONS

There are three places where we handle the Nanonaut's animation: **CONSTANTS**, the **update()** function, and the **draw()** function. If we look at the Nanonaut drawing code in the **draw()** function, we see this:

```
var nanonautSpriteSheetRow = Math.floor(nanonautFrameNr /
NANONAUT_NR_FRAMES_PER_ROW);
var nanonautSpriteSheetColumn = nanonautFrameNr % NANONAUT_NR_FRAMES_PER_ROW;
var nanonautSpriteSheetX = nanonautSpriteSheetColumn * NANONAUT_WIDTH;
var nanonautSpriteSheetY = nanonautSpriteSheetRow * NANONAUT_HEIGHT;
c.drawImage(nanonautImage, // The Nanonaut spritesheet.
nanonautSpriteSheetX, nanonautSpriteSheetY, // Coordinates within spritesheet.
NANONAUT_WIDTH, NANONAUT_HEIGHT, // The size of the frame in the spritesheet.
nanonautX - cameraX, nanonautY - cameraY, // The position on-screen.
NANONAUT_WIDTH, NANONAUT_HEIGHT // The size on-screen.
);
```

What's Nanonaut-specific about this? On the one hand, variables (which animation frame, which coordinates, which image). On the other hand, constants (**NANONAUT_NR_FRAMES_PER_ROW**, etc.).

But those constants all belong together with the spritesheet. So what if we make an object that bundles everything we need to know about the spritesheet and use that? Like so:

Add this in your **SETUP** code, after loading the images.

```
var nanonautSpriteSheet = {
nrFramesPerRow: 5,
spriteWidth: NANONAUT_WIDTH,
spriteHeight: NANONAUT_HEIGHT,
image: nanonautImage
};
```

We can then make a function that draws any animated sprite. Add this at the end of your **draw()** function:

```
//Draw Animated Sprite
function drawAnimatedSprite(screenX, screenY, frameNr, spriteSheet) {
var spriteSheetRow = Math.floor(frameNr / spriteSheet.nrFramesPerRow);
var spriteSheetColumn = frameNr % spriteSheet.nrFramesPerRow;
var spriteSheetX = spriteSheetColumn * spriteSheet.spriteWidth;
var spriteSheetY = spriteSheetRow * spriteSheet.spriteHeight;
c.drawImage(
spriteSheet.image,
spriteSheetX, spriteSheetY,
spriteSheet.spriteWidth, spriteSheet.spriteHeight, screenX, screenY,
spriteSheet.spriteWidth, spriteSheet.spriteHeight
);
}
```

Delete the **NANONAUT_NR_FRAMES_PER_ROW** from your **CONSTANTS** section: We don't need it anymore.

Create a completely new image called **robotImage** that loads **animatedRobot.png**, in your **SETUP** section, as we did before.

Add these to your
CONSTANTS:

```
var ROBOT_WIDTH = 141;
var ROBOT_HEIGHT = 139;
```

Add this code to make a robot spritesheet in your **SETUP** section:

```
var bush2Image = new Image();
bush2Image.src = 'bush2.png';

var robotImage = new Image();
robotImage.src = 'animatedRobot.png';

var robotSpriteSheet = {
nrFramesPerRow: 3,
spriteWidth: ROBOT_WIDTH,
spriteHeight: ROBOT_HEIGHT,
image: robotImage
};
```

And right after that, a small list of robots for testing, like this:

```
var robotData = [{
x: 400,
y: GROUND_Y - ROBOT_HEIGHT,
frameNr: 0
}];
```

Then we replace the Nanonaut drawing code and add a robot drawing code in **draw()** like so:

```
// Draw the bushes.
for (var i=0; i<bushData.length; i++) {
c.drawImage(bushData[i].image, bushData[i].x - cameraX, GROUND_Y -
bushData[i].y - cameraY);
}

// Draw the robots.
for (var i=0; i<robotData.length; i++) {
drawAnimatedSprite(robotData[i].x - cameraX,
robotData[i].y - cameraY, robotData[i].frameNr, robotSpriteSheet);
}

// Draw the Nanonaut.
drawAnimatedSprite(nanonautX - cameraX, nanonautY - cameraY,
nanonautFrameNr, nanonautSpriteSheet);
}
```

Try it now! You should see a robot.

ANIMATING ROBOTS

Now to animate the robot. We need to loop over all of the robots and do the animation logic we've already done for the Nanonaut. This has to happen inside the update function. But because we're going to do a lot more logic for each robot, we're going to move all of that into a function. Add this to the end of the **update()** function:

```
// Update bushes.
for (var i=0; i<bushData.length; i++) {
if ((bushData[i].x - cameraX) < -CANVAS_WIDTH) {
bushData[i].x += (2 * CANVAS_WIDTH) + 150;
}
}

// Update robots.
updateRobots();
}


function updateRobots() {
// Move and animate robots.
for (var i=0; i<robotData.length; i++) {
if ((gameFrameCounter % ROBOT_ANIMATION_SPEED) === 0) {
robotData[i].frameNr = robotData[i].frameNr + 1;
if (robotData[i].frameNr >= ROBOT_NR_ANIMATION_FRAMES) {
robotData[i].frameNr = 0;
}
}
}
}
```

Before this new code will work, you need to add new constants – **ROBOT_NR_ANIMATION_FRAMES** (with a value of 9) and **ROBOT_ANIMATION_SPEED** (with a value of 5) – to the **CONSTANTS** section.

Shouldn't the animation speed or the number of frames be part of the spritesheet? No, because we might put more than one animation in a spritesheet.

So, where were we? "Evil animated robots running from right to left."

Running! Right. It's just like for the Nanonaut. Add just one line to the code you wrote above:

```
for (var i=0; i<robotData.length; i++) {
robotData[i].x -= ROBOT_X_SPEED;
if ((gameFrameCounter % ROBOT_ANIMATION_SPEED) === 0) {
```

Finally, define the **ROBOT_X_SPEED** constant. Set it to 4: Robots are not as fast as Nanonauts. Try it!

7. Evil animated robots running from right to left.

Well, there's only one robot. And it runs to the left ... and keeps running ... and never comes back.

What we really want is for a robot to run all the way to the left, then disappear, and then a new one appears on the right. It's a bit like what we've done for the bushes, except this time we're not going to just move the same robots back to the right: We're going to actually remove the robot on the left and generate a new one on the right. So could we do something like this?

```
for (var i=0; i<robotData.length; i++) {
if (...robot is too far left..) {
...delete robot somehow...
}
```

Nope. Let's see what that would do. We would start with:

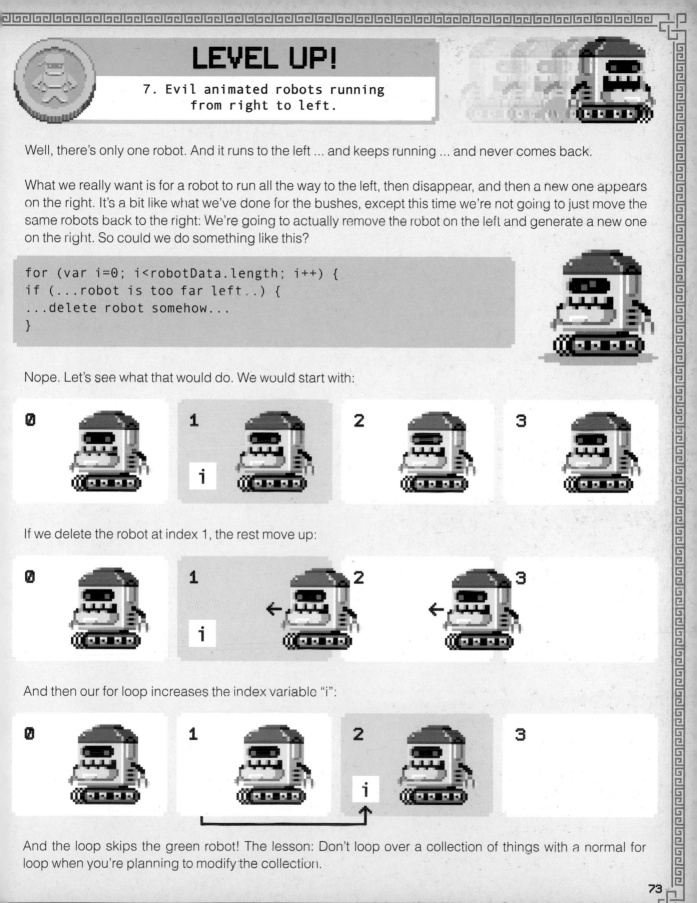

If we delete the robot at index 1, the rest move up:

And then our for loop increases the index variable "i":

And the loop skips the green robot! The lesson: Don't loop over a collection of things with a normal for loop when you're planning to modify the collection.

UPDATING ROBOTS

Instead, we're going to use a **while** loop, to go through the robots and see if any should be removed. Put this at the end of your **updateRobots** function:

```
robotData[i].frameNr = 0;
}
}
}
// Remove robots that have gone off-screen.
var robotIndex = 0;
while (robotIndex < robotData.length) {
if (robotData[robotIndex].x < cameraX - ROBOT_WIDTH) {
robotData.splice(robotIndex, 1);
console.log("I removed a robot!");
} else {
robotIndex += 1;
}
}
```

Before we look at that in more detail, run it. You should see the message "I removed a robot!" in the console. That tells us the code seems to work, so you can take the **console.log()** line out again.

OK, but how does this work? Instead of having the for command increase the index for us, we're doing it manually, and only when we're not deleting a robot. This way, we never skip a robot!

The condition we use to check if a robot is off-screen should be clear. But what is this **splice** command?

```
robotData.splice(robotIndex, 1);
```

This says "Remove a part of the array, starting at **robotIndex**, with a length of 1." This is how we remove elements from an array.

So how and when do we add new robots? Let's say we want a certain number of robots to be active at the same time, and, a bit like with bushes, we want there to be a minimum and a maximum distance between them. Add these variables to the **CONSTANTS**:

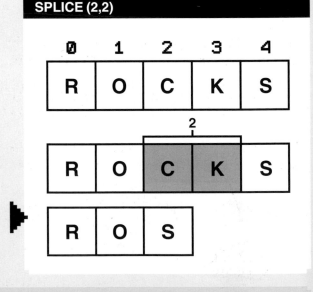

SPLICE (2,2)

0	1	2	3	4
R	O	C	K	S

2

R	O	C	K	S

R	O	S

```
var MIN_DISTANCE_BETWEEN_ROBOTS = 400;
var MAX_DISTANCE_BETWEEN_ROBOTS = 1200;
var MAX_ACTIVE_ROBOTS = 3;
```

We're going to be using some of these numbers more than once, so we're using constants.

Then, at the end of **updateRobots()**, add:

```
robotData.splice(robotIndex, 1);
console.log("I removed a robot!");
} else {
robotIndex += 1;
}
}


if (robotData.length < MAX_ACTIVE_ROBOTS) {
var lastRobotX = robotData[robotData.length - 1].x;
var newRobotX = lastRobotX + MIN_DISTANCE_BETWEEN_ROBOTS + Math.random() *
(MAX_DISTANCE_BETWEEN_ROBOTS - MIN_DISTANCE_BETWEEN_ROBOTS);
robotData.push({
x: newRobotX,
y: GROUND_Y - ROBOT_HEIGHT,
frameNr: 0
});
}
```

So we're saying "If there aren't enough active robots, take the X coordinate of the last robot, then add a random distance to it and generate a new robot there." Note how we didn't randomize the Y coordinate or the animation frame, because they're robots.

Try it. Looks fine, right? Yes, except there's a potential bug. Make a change to your **robotData** in the **SETUP** section to:

```
var robotData = [];
```

After all, we have our fancy robot logic now, so we don't need that data anymore, right? Wrong. Run it, and you may see an error message like this in the console:

```
updateRobots :TypeError: undefined
is not an object (evaluating
'robotData[robotData.length - 1].x')
```

Yikes! What the browser is clumsily trying to tell us is that it can't calculate **robotData[robotData.length -1].x**. And the reason is that **robotData** is empty, so **robotData.length** is 0, and we're telling it to get the element at index - 1. And that was never going to end well.

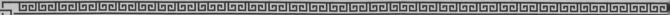

DEFENSIVE PROGRAMMING

We assumed the array wouldn't be empty, but we were wrong! It's time for more defensive programming! Try changing the **lastRobotX** line, and add an if statement to fix this:

```
if (robotData.length < MAX_ACTIVE_ROBOTS) {
var lastRobotX = 0;
if (robotData.length > 0) {
lastRobotX = robotData[robotData.length - 1].x;
}
```

That should work. Try it out!

Uh-oh. If you run the game a couple of times, you will see that sometimes the first robot is generated much too far on the left. And that's unfair for the player: They have no chance to avoid the robot.

Do you see why this happens? We're saying "If there are no robots, assume the last one has an X coordinate of 0." But really we should pick a much higher value. Make this change:

```
if (robotData.length < MAX_ACTIVE_ROBOTS) {
var lastRobotX = CANVAS_WIDTH;
if (robotData.length > 0) {
```

Now everything works fine.

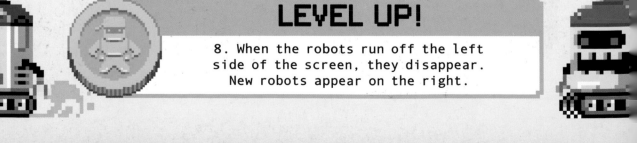

LEVEL UP!

8. When the robots run off the left side of the screen, they disappear. New robots appear on the right.

COLLISION DETECTION

Now we're going to make the Nanonaut lose health when they come in contact with a robot.

First, we need to find out when a Nanonaut touches a robot. The fancy game programming word for this is **collision detection**. It's not easy, but we can solve it by working our way through step by step.

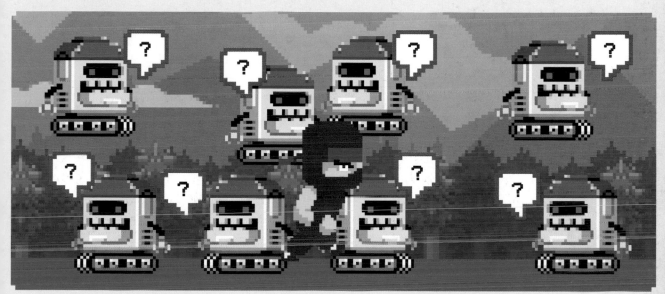

It's possible to do very precise (sometimes called **pixel perfect**) collision detection, but often we can get a result that's good enough by solving a much easier problem. So what we're going to do is look at the rectangles around the robot and the Nanonaut. These are called **bounding boxes**.

The ones we'll be using are called **axis-aligned bounding boxes**, and they're great for us to work with.

Now, there is a problem. When the shape of the Nanonaut or robot doesn't fill out the bounding box, our approach will say there's a collision when in fact there isn't.

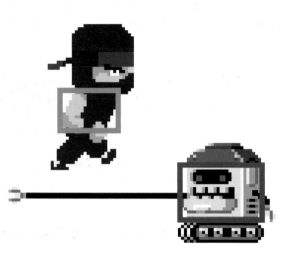

This is going to feel very unfair to the player. If we're going to make mistakes, we should try to make mistakes that are in favor of the player. What if we use boxes that are smaller?

So, strictly speaking, these aren't bounding boxes anymore. Let's call them **collision rectangles**.

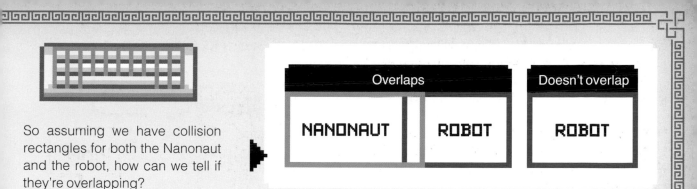

So assuming we have collision rectangles for both the Nanonaut and the robot, how can we tell if they're overlapping?

Overlaps		Doesn't overlap
NANONAUT	ROBOT	ROBOT

Again, we can make our problem easier by breaking it down into two smaller problems. Instead of trying to solve everything at once, we'll look at the X-axis and Y-axis separately. The rectangles overlap when they overlap both horizontally and vertically.

So how do we detect if two rectangles overlap horizontally? There are two obvious cases:

Because we're only looking at one axis at a time, we can detect these cases with simple comparisons, like we've already done:

```
if ((nanonautRightX >= robotLeftX) && (nanonautRightX <= robotRightX)) { …

if ((nanonautLeftX >= robotLeftX) && (nanonautLeftX <= robotRightX)) { …
```

COLLISION LOGIC

There's another case we need to think of:

Our current logic wouldn't catch this case. So we need one more check:

```
if ((nanonautLeftX <= robotLeftX) && (nanonautRightX >= robotRightX)) { …
```

We need to do those three checks, and if either one of them is true, the Nanonaut overlaps the robot horizontally. Then we do the same checks for the vertical axis, and if the Nanonaut overlaps there too, we have a collision. Phew! So how do we actually structure the program?

Again, we want to use functions to break down our code into nice and simple parts. The smallest building block we have is the three cases we identified, so why don't we put that into a function? And let's try to make it work for both the horizontal and the vertical axis: We can talk about "near" and "far" instead of "left" and "right"; that will also work for the vertical axis.

Before we write the code, let's look at the if statement again:

```
if (...condition...) {
...execute this when the condition is true...
} else {
...execute this when the condition is false...
}
```

As we saw on page 43, boolean variables can also be true or false. Are these two things related? Yes! Because we can also write:

```
var isSomethingTrue = ...condition...;
if (isSomethingTrue) {
...execute this when the condition is true...
} else {
...execute this when the condition is false...
}
```

In our case, we have three conditions that all consist of other conditions that have been combined using the logical and operator. We could combine all that into one big if statement, but it would involve a *lot* of parentheses. So let's use boolean variables instead:

```
function doesNanonautOverlapRobotAlongOneAxis(nanonautNearX, nanonautFarX,
robotNearX, robotFarX) {
var nanonautOverlapsNearRobotEdge = (nanonautFarX >= robotNearX) &&
(nanonautFarX <= robotFarX);
var nanonautOverlapsFarRobotEdge = (nanonautNearX >= robotNearX) &&
(nanonautNearX <= robotFarX);
var nanonautOverlapsEntireRobot = (nanonautNearX <= robotNearX) &&
(nanonautFarX >= robotFarX);
return nanonautOverlapsNearRobotEdge || nanonautOverlapsFarRobotEdge ||
nanonautOverlapsEntireRobot;
}
```

Add that after the **updateRobots()** function.

Note that we are using the **logical or operator**, which is written as ||. At the end, we're simply saying "If the first or the second or the third boolean variable is true, return true, otherwise false."

Also note that we're using long-but-clear function and variable names to help us understand what is going on.

NINJA TIP

The character used in the logical or operator can be found above the backslash on a keyboard.

Now that we have programmed the logic at the heart of collision detection, let's build another function on top of it that actually looks at the Nanonaut and robot data on both axes:

```
return nanonautOverlapsNearRobotEdge || nanonautOverlapsFarRobotEdge ||
nanonautOverlapsEntireRobot;
}
function doesNanonautOverlapRobot(nanonautX, nanonautY, nanonautWidth,
nanonautHeight, robotX, robotY, robotWidth, robotHeight) {
var nanonautOverlapsRobotOnXAxis = doesNanonautOverlapRobotAlongOneAxis(
nanonautX,
nanonautX + nanonautWidth,
robotX,
robotX + robotWidth
);
var nanonautOverlapsRobotOnYAxis = doesNanonautOverlapRobotAlongOneAxis(
nanonautY,
nanonautY + nanonautHeight,
robotY,
robotY + robotHeight
);
return nanonautOverlapsRobotOnXAxis && nanonautOverlapsRobotOnYAxis;
}
```

You may be wondering why this function has the Nanonaut's coordinates as parameters. Don't we have that in a variable already? Don't we have all these parameters in other variables already?

There are two reasons. First of all, we're going to detect collisions using collision rectangles that are smaller than the sprite we're drawing. We don't know where those rectangles will be coming from, but they won't be the same as what's in our existing variables.

But second, you should be careful about having functions use global variables. It's almost always better when functions use parameters instead. This way, whenever we want to change those variables, we don't need to worry about changing dozens of functions. For example: What if we were to add a second Nanonaut? With the function above, that'd be easy. If that function were to use **nanonautX** directly, it'd be much harder. Things get even worse when functions can change variables. Suddenly a variable changes, and we have to search our entire program to find out who did it! As programs grow, this becomes more and more important.

So where will those collision rectangles come from? We know we will need one for the Nanonaut and one for the robot. We also know we need four values to define a rectangle. So this sounds like a job for an object! Let's add this to our **SETUP** section, after the spritesheet data:

The offsets tell us whether the rectangles are from the Nanonaut's or robot's positions.

Now to actually call our collision logic. In your **updateRobots()** function, inside the loop where we update the robots, write:

```
var nanonautCollisionRectangle = {
xOffset: 60,
yOffset: 20,
width: 50,
height: 200
};
var robotCollisionRectangle = {
xOffset: 50,
yOffset: 20,
width: 50,
height: 100
};
```

```
for (var i=0; i<robotData.length; i++) {
if (doesNanonautOverlapRobot(
nanonautX + nanonautCollisionRectangle.xOffset,
nanonautY + nanonautCollisionRectangle.yOffset,
nanonautCollisionRectangle.width,
nanonautCollisionRectangle.height,
robotData[i].x + robotCollisionRectangle.xOffset,
robotData[i].y + robotCollisionRectangle.yOffset,
robotCollisionRectangle.width,
robotCollisionRectangle.height
)) {
console.log('OUCH!');
}
robotData[i].x -= ROBOT_X_SPEED;
```

We haven't decided yet what we're going to do when the Nanonaut touches a robot, so we just log something to the console to see if the code works. Try it out, and make sure to have the console open. You should see "OUCH!" when the Nanonaut touches a robot.

OUCH!

>

SCREEN SHAKE

But what do we really want to show to the player when the Nanonaut touches the robot? Let's make the screen shake!

Making the screen shake is easy; we just need to move the camera around a bit. Except when the screen shake stops, the camera should be back where it was. The screen shake has to be relative to the camera's position.

To do this we're going to add the following code to the start of our draw function:

```
// Shake the screen if necessary.
var shakenCameraX = cameraX;
var shakenCameraY = cameraY;

if (screenshake) {
// TO DO: Change shakenCameraX and Y to make the camera shake
}
```

Be sure to add the screenshake variable to your **SETUP** section. Set it to false.

Now make the rest of the draw function – the code to draw the background, the bushes, the robots, and the Nanonaut – use **shakenCameraX** and **shakenCameraY** instead of **cameraX** and **cameraY**.

For instance, this ...

```
// Draw the bushes.
for (var i=0; i<bushData.length; i++)
{
c.drawImage(bushData[i].image,
bushData[i].x - cameraX, GROUND_Y -
bushData[i].y - cameraY);
}
```

... becomes:

```
// Draw the bushes.
for (var i=0; i<bushData.length; i++)
{
c.drawImage(bushData[i].image,
bushData[i].x - shakenCameraX, GROUND_Y -
bushData[i].y - shakenCameraY);
}
```

Do you see how much harder this would be if we had used the global variables **cameraX** and **cameraY** everywhere? This is why **drawAnimatedSprite** takes coordinates in screen space, not world space.

Now we have to shake the camera. To do that, we need random numbers again. Add this to your **CONSTANTS**:

```
var SCREENSHAKE_RADIUS = 16;
```

We then want to make sure the camera shakes in all directions, not just forward and up. So we need to make sure the range of the random numbers goes from -8 to 8, instead of 0 to 16. Then we can replace the **TO DO** we wrote earlier with this:

```
if (screenshake) {
shakenCameraX += (Math.random() - .5) * SCREENSHAKE_RADIUS;
shakenCameraY += (Math.random() - .5) * SCREENSHAKE_RADIUS;
}
```

This first shifts the range from -0.5 to 0.5, then multiplies it with the radius to get to -8 to 8. Now all we need to do is turn the screen shake on or off. The place where we know that the Nanonaut touched a robot is inside **updateRobots**. But is that where we want to turn on screen shake? Should the function that updates robots have to know about screen shake, and the Nanonaut health logic that will come next? No. We should keep those things separate, so each line of code is focused on one thing.

The screen shake and the health logic, which we'll get to in a moment, are better placed in the update function. So we need a way for **updateRobots** to tell **update()** that the Nanonaut touched a robot. We could use a global variable for that, but as we've seen, global variables are a bit iffy. There's a better way: We're going to use the **return** command to send a value back to whoever called **updateRobots**.

Inside **updateRobots**, make these changes:

```
// Move and animate robots and check collision with Nanonaut.
var nanonautTouchedARobot = false;
for (var i=0; i<robotData.length; i++) {
if (doesNanonautOverlapRobot(
nanonautX + nanonautCollisionRectangle.xOffset,
nanonautY + nanonautCollisionRectangle.yOffset,
nanonautCollisionRectangle.width,
nanonautCollisionRectangle.height,
robotData[i].x + robotCollisionRectangle.xOffset,
robotData[i].y + robotCollisionRectangle.yOffset,
robotCollisionRectangle.width,
robotCollisionRectangle.height
)) {
nanonautTouchedARobot = true;
}
```

Note how the condition of the if statement here is the return value of the **doesNanonautOverlapRobot** function, which returns a boolean value. It looks scarier than it is.

At the very end of **updateRobots**, add:

```
    return nanonautTouchedARobot;
}
```

PLAYER HEALTH

Now change the function call for **updateRobots** inside **update()** from:

```
updateRobots();
```

to

```
screenshake = false;
var nanonautTouchedARobot = updateRobots();
if (nanonautTouchedARobot) {
screenshake = true;
}
```

As you can see, you can use the return value of **updateRobots** as if it were any other value or variable.

Now the screen should shake whenever the Nanonaut hits a robot.

We're nearly there! Let's keep track of the Nanonaut's health. Add this to your **CONSTANTS**:

```
var NANONAUT_MAX_HEALTH = 100;
```

Then add this variable to your **SETUP** section:

```
var nanonautHealth = NANONAUT_MAX_HEALTH;
```

Then at the end of the **update()** function, change this:

```
if (nanonautTouchedARobot) {
screenshake = true;
if (nanonautHealth > 0) nanonautHealth -= 1;
}
```

Very simple, right? Touch a robot, lose one point of health.

Now we need to make sure the player knows their health. Let's add a health bar. Add the following after the Nanonaut drawing code:

```
// Draw the Nanonaut.
drawAnimatedSprite(nanonautX - shakenCameraX, nanonautY -
shakenCameraY, nanonautFrameNr, nanonautSpriteSheet);

// Draw the health bar.
c.fillStyle = 'red';
c.fillRect(400, 10, nanonautHealth / NANONAUT_MAX_HEALTH * 380, 20);
}
```

We divide the Nanonaut's health by its maximum health to get the relative health. Then we multiply it with the width of the full health bar. This way we spread the relative health over the width of the bar.

It's hard to see how full the health bar is right now, and when the Nanonaut's health is 0, there is nothing left on-screen. So let's add an empty rectangle behind the bar using **strokeRect**.

```
c.strokeStyle = 'red';
c.strokeRect(400, 10, 380, 20);
```

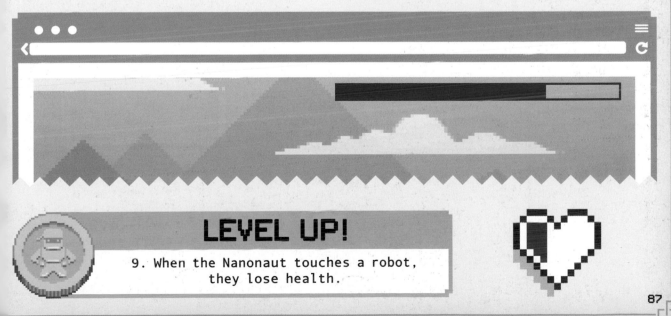

LEVEL UP!

9. When the Nanonaut touches a robot,
they lose health.

Our game is working well, but it doesn't stop when the Nanonaut's health has dropped to zero. We want everything to stop moving and for the game to say "GAME OVER" in nice, big letters.

To do this we need to keep track of a **mode**. When the game is running normally, we're in "play mode," and when the game is over, we're in "game over mode." It is normal for games to have lots and lots of modes, both for the entire game and for individual elements. For example, when a boss enemy in a game becomes angry and does more damage, that's a mode. When you press pause, that's a mode. Keeping track of all of these modes can get complicated.

But we're going to keep things simple for now. We'll just implement modes for the entire game and give each mode a number, using constants, of course:

```
var PLAY_GAME_MODE = 0;
var GAME_OVER_GAME_MODE = 1;
```

Then we add this variable to your **SETUP** section:

```
var gameMode = PLAY_GAME_MODE;
```

Then, at the start of our update function, we say:

```
function update() {
if (gameMode != PLAY_GAME_MODE) return;
```

We add that because we don't need to update anything when the game is over. At the end of update, add:

```
if (nanonautHealth > 0) nanonautHealth -= 1;
}
 // Check if the game is over.
if (nanonautHealth <= 0) {
gameMode = GAME_OVER_GAME_MODE;
}
}
```

NINJA TIP

You can temporarily set the Nanonaut's maximum health to 10 to make it easier to test.

Now try it out! What did you see? That's right, the screen shaking never stops when the Nanonaut's health becomes zero. Do you understand why?

It's easy to fix—make this change at the end of your **update()** function:

```
if (nanonautHealth <= 0) {
gameMode = GAME_OVER_GAME_MODE;
screenshake = false;
}
```

Now to display "GAME OVER." We draw text using the **fillText** API function. It takes a string, an X coordinate, and a Y coordinate.

So at the end of your draw function (do you know why it has to be at the end?), add:

```
// If the game is over, draw "GAME OVER."
if (gameMode == GAME_OVER_GAME_MODE) {
c.fillStyle = 'black';
c.fillText('GAME OVER', 120, 300);
}
}


//Draw Animated Sprite
```

If you try it out, you will see it's ... not very dramatic. We need to tell the browser to use bigger letters. Just like with the stroke color, we do that with a special function that we call before drawing the text:

```
if (gameMode == GAME_OVER_GAME_MODE) {
c.fillStyle = 'black';
c.font = '96px sans-serif';
c.fillText('GAME OVER', 120, 300);
}
```

We're saying "Please use a sans-serif font that is 96 pixels high from now on." Sans-serif fonts tend to be clean and modern looking. It actually doesn't really matter which kind of font we use, but the browser insists we say something.

LEVEL UP!

10. When the Nanonaut has lost all health, the game stops.

SCORING

All we need to do now is tell the player how far they've run, so they can try to run as far as they can and compare scores with friends. We know how far the Nanonaut has come in pixels, but players don't care about pixels. We're not going to think too hard about how big the Nanonaut is—we'll just use something that feels right. We'll say that 100 pixels is 1 meter.

At the end of the draw function, before the code that draws the health bar, add:

```
// Draw the distance the Nanonaut has traveled.
var nanonautDistance = nanonautX / 100;
c.fillStyle = 'black';
c.font = '48px sans-serif';
c.fillText(nanonautDistance.toFixed(0) + 'm', 20, 40);

// Draw the Nanonaut's health bar.
c.strokeStyle = 'red';
```

We're using two tricks here. We're using the **toFixed(0)** API function to convert the number from something like 230.45344 into the string "230." The parameter 0 says we want 0 positions after the period, because we don't care about decimeters or centimeters.

The other trick is we're using addition to combine two strings: the converted number and the "m" to indicate the distance is in meters. Practical, isn't it?

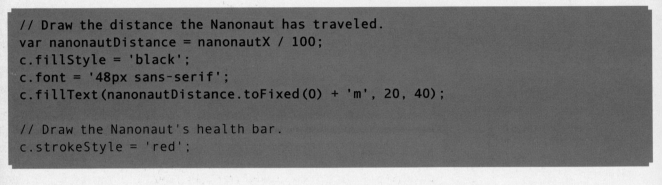

230m ←

957205(392)
71033392817
.0182%21019
(09724.6)97
3571998_328

LEVEL COMPLETE!

1. ~~We see a Nanonaut in an exciting world.~~

2. ~~The Nanonaut will fall to the ground.~~

3. ~~The Nanonaut can jump into the air.~~

4. ~~The Nanonaut automatically runs to the right, followed by the camera.~~

5. ~~The Nanonaut is animated.~~

6. ~~There are background objects, to make the world more lively.~~

7. ~~Evil animated robots run from right to left.~~

8. ~~When the robots run off the left side of the screen, they disappear.~~
   ~~New robots appear on the right.~~

9. ~~When the Nanonaut touches a robot, they lose health.~~

10. ~~When the Nanonaut has lost all health, the game stops.~~

MORE ONLINE

To play the completed game, head to scholastic.com/coder-dojo/nanonautjump

If you want to check your code, you can find the full document at scholastic.com/coder-dojo/indentation

CONTINUE?

TAKING THE GAME FURTHER

Here are some ideas for things you can add to the game yourself:

Add Nano Tokens that the player can collect. Nano Tokens are drawn like bushes, but you need to check for collisions, remove the token, and increase a counter whenever the player touches one. Then you need to display that counter somewhere so the player knows how many tokens they've collected.

On the game-over screen, display the final distance and number of tokens the player has achieved.

Make the game harder by making the robots run faster, or the Nanonaut jump less high.

Make the Nanonaut slide when the player presses the cursor down key. You will probably have to make a new animation—see the next page for how to do that.

Add new enemies that fly, so the player has to slide under them.

Instead of always making all enemies advance with the same speed inside **updateRobots()**, store the function that updates the enemy inside the robot object, like a callback. That way, you can make enemies that have completely different behaviors.

You can do the same for collisions. Store the function that reacts to the collision in the robot object. That way you can make robots that throw the Nanonaut into the air or restore health.

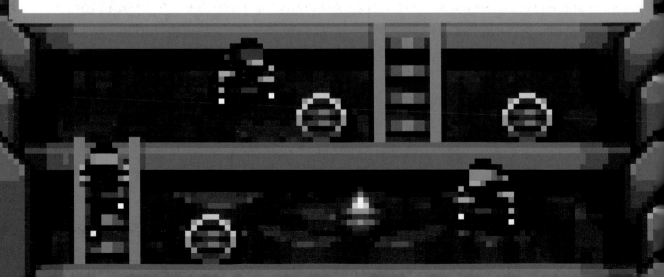

MAKING YOUR OWN IMAGES

If you want to make your own images, here are some tips!

You can either adapt the images we have provided, try to make your own, or look for images on the Internet.

You can use **image-editing programs** like Microsoft Paint, GNU Image Manipulation Program (GIMP), or others to make or adapt images.

We recommend using the **JPG** or **PNG** image formats. You can tell from the file extension which format an image uses: `background.png` uses the **PNG** format, for instance.

When you change the image format or the image file name, don't forget to change the code that loads the images in the **SETUP** section. If you create a new background image called `mountains.jpg`, you need to replace the `background.png` code with `mountains.jpg`.

Background

Bushes

Robots and Nanonauts

Sky and ground

All of the images should have an **alpha channel**, meaning they can be partially transparent. Without that, you would see empty white rectangles around everything.

The background should be an image at least as wide as the canvas, so in our case 800 pixels wide or more. The height is less important. Be sure to change **BACKGROUND_WIDTH** based on the width of your image, and of course you will have to tweak the drawing code inside your **draw()** function.

The bushes can be any size you want. They don't have to be just bushes: They can be any kind of decorative object. You've seen how we added the second bush on page 63; you can add more objects the same way. You'll have to adapt **generateBushes()** if the objects have different widths and heights, though.

For the robots and Nanonauts, make sure all the individual sprites in the spritesheets have the same size. Adapt the **CONSTANTS** (**ROBOT_WIDTH** etc.), as well as the spritesheet objects and the collision rectangle objects in your **SETUP** section.

AFTERWORD

Congratulations on programming your first game! You've done much more than that, though. You've mastered the power of JavaScript, and JavaScript can be used to create much more than games. In *CoderDojo Nano: Build Your Own Website*, I wrote about the history of programming – now you are the future of it!

You can create apps for smartphones that do almost anything you can imagine. You can also much more easily learn other scripting languages, which are capable of doing a huge variety of things. From robotics to drone control, scripting languages can even reprogram life these days, with languages like Antha revolutionizing the world of biology. It is all at your fingertips.

Now you are getting good, stay with it and keep giving yourself new challenges. More importantly meet up with other young coders like you in your friendship circle, or at a local CoderDojo. If there is no local CoderDojo, get together with some friends and their parents and start one. You now know enough to lead a Dojo Nano, and the only thing better than a great coder is a team of great coders. Coderdojo.com is for you. Amaze us with what you and your friends build together.

— Bill Liao, CoderDojo Foundation